THE ROYAL MARINES

THE ROYAL MARINES

A DOCUMENTARY BY

JOHN ROBERT YOUNG

GUILD PUBLISHING

LONDON · NEW YORK · SYDNEY · TORONTO

This book is for Pam and Jenny who, between them, gave the project a nudge in the right direction.

This edition published 1991 by Guild Publishing by arrangement with Doubleday a division of Transworld Publishers Ltd
CN 6822

Typeset by Tradespools Ltd, Frome, Somerset
Printed in Great Britain by
BPCC Hazell Books, Paulton and Aylesbury

Right: The 3rd Raiding Squadron on patrol off the Hong Kong coast.

CONTENTS

Acknowledgements 6
Introduction 7

1 IRELAND 9
The Marines at War, Belfast   10
The Padre   25
The Women and the Corps   27

2 TRAINING: Some are Chosen but Few Succeed 29
The Recruiting Office   32
Lympstone: Commando Training
    Centre   33
The Brigade Air Squadron   48
Snipers   54

3 TO THE FAR ENDS OF THE EARTH: From the South China Sea to the South Atlantic 57
The Hong Kong Connection   58
Norway: Guarding the Northern
    Flank   70
The Falklands   80

4 THE WORLD IS OUR STAGE 89
Beating Retreat: Whitehall,
    London   90
The School of Music   98
The Christmas Pantomime   116

5 THE LEADERS 121
The Generals   122
The Officers   132
The NCOs   142
After the Corps   148

Conclusion, and the Way Ahead   157
Historical Section   161
Select Bibliography   188
Photographic Notes   188
Index   189

Acknowledgements

Gaining access to any military community is never easy. Asking to be allowed to roam free with camera and tape recorder is in most circumstances nigh impossible, for in recent years our Armed Forces have become increasingly suspicious of the media. In some quarters, mention of press or journalist, whoever they may be and from whatever hallowed institution, is met at the very least with suspicion; more often than not with resentment and hostility.

In some quarters, eyebrows were raised within the Corps when I was accredited and given complete freedom to produce this book. I would therefore especially like to pay tribute to Lieutenant-General Sir Martin Garrod, KCB, OBE, Commandant-General of the Marines at the time I commenced in 1987, who gave his permission and complete support for the project. Similarly, I am indebted to his successor, Lieutenant-General Beverley, OBE, the present Commandant-General, and to Major-General Ross, OBE, Major-General Vaux, CB, DSO, and Major-General Whitehead, DSO for their enthusiasm throughout.

As with many things in the uncertain, yet enthralling, world of publishing and journalism, the proposal for this book was hatched over lunch, with a former Lieutenant-Colonel of Marines. Terry Knott, holder of the Military Cross and a Falklands veteran, was my first contact with the Corps. At all times sensitive to my needs and problems, he helped to smooth the way and obtain the help of everyone during my early days with the Marines.

Throughout my travels I was accompanied by members of the Royal Marines public relations team. Their help and counsel were invaluable, always extending well beyond the call of duty. At the most opportune moments, whether in the Scottish Highlands, Norway or Sardinia, liquid nourishment would appear from knapsacks as well as tasty morsels from ration packs. Ever cheerful and resourceful, they assisted me in numerous ways to secure my pictures and text. I shall always retain fond memories of my time with them, and wish to thank the following: Warrant Officer John Nicholson, at Lympstone; Colour Sergeant John Kimbrey, in Scotland and Sardinia; Colour Sergeant Nigel Devenish, in Norway; Sergeant Steve Sugden, in the Falklands and the UK; and Sergeant Al Heward, in Northern Ireland. Ever willing to assist were three Royal Navy photographers: Petty Officers Ric Birch, Al Campbell and Fez Parker.

Behind the scenes there were many others, too numerous to mention, including Captain Hank de Jaeger, Captain Ian Grant, Captain Mike Buffine, Captain Joe House, Lieutenant Nick Bentham-Green, former Fleet RSM 'Black Jock' Gordon, the President of the Sergeants' mess at Lympstone, Warrant Officer RSM Keith Anderson, who always made me a welcome guest, and Warrant Officer Brian Evans. Four former members of the Corps, who kindly reminisced about their lives in and out of the Marines, were Corporal 'Bill' Sparks, DSM, of Cockleshell Hero fame, Warrant Officer John Kirtley, Corporal Dave Morris and Marine David 'Spudge' Swayne. I am also indebted to the staff of the Royal Marines Museum at Eastney, especially Andy Lane, the curator, Matthew Little, librarian, and Edwin Bartholomew, photographic librarian, for their invaluable help in researching material for the historical section of this book.

Books such as this have much in common with the documentary film. It is a team effort that places the book on the world's bookshelves. I would like to thank Belinda Flood for finalizing my text on the word processor, Jenny Barrett for editing, filing and indexing thousands of transparencies, Mandy Greenfield for diligently shaping my text and Philip Gilderdale for his patient understanding and translation of my feelings on design and layout.

My final debt of gratitude is to those hundreds of Royal Marines, of all ranks, with whom I spoke. Without their participation none of this would have been possible.

John Robert Young
Lewes, Sussex
March 1991

INTRODUCTION

In our compulsive, consumer-oriented society, which is fast losing its direction, becoming fat and pot-bellied, where discipline is scorned and the scramble for wealth is foremost in the minds of our youth, the green beret of the Royal Marine Commandos stands alone as being a rare pearl of great price. It is a symbol of excellence, dedication and professionalism; an accolade for those who push themselves beyond the limits of normal human endurance. In an age when standards are crumbling, the green beret is as British as the Union Jack, for it represents true grit and dogged individual determination. The green beret is not for sale – though some may have been won by more sweat and assiduity than others. Thousands have sought to attain it, but along the way many have wilted and failed. It is a classless symbol of fortitude and achievement.

Most Britons are oblivious to the role of the Marine Corps in peacetime, beyond that of Marine bands playing at public or civic functions around the world. True, one hears of them on the streets of Belfast, and their exploits in the Falklands campaign are legendary. Apart from these instances, however, there is a void. Our Royal Marines are sometimes perceived as an extension of the British Tourist Board, since so little is understood of their comings and goings. Compared to our forefathers, who fairly revelled in a mixture of nationalism, the regiment and Elgar, the British public nowadays has an understandable ambivalence towards all things military. Cries of 'rally to the flag, boys' have a poor following these days. Our world is entering a new age and, thankfully, politicians are talking of 'turning tanks into tractors'. The Cold War and the Soviet menace are yesteryear's fears. Revolution has swept across Europe, which will never be the same again. How true the words of Mao Tse-tung, who wrote that 'a revolution is not a dinner party. . .'

With declining numbers entering the Armed Forces, and anxious budget-masters being far from euphoric about the zero-growth defence spending constraints, is it possible that institutions like the Royal Marines might suffer cutbacks, military 'mothballing' or, worst of all, be rendered obsolete? True, the Falklands was an epic victory, but as old soldiers know, time dims the memory. As far as the Corps is concerned, it sees no reason to question its future. Marines are never pessimists. 'Let's go for it!' is their battle cry. They see themselves as the spearhead of Britain's defences. Obsolescence is for others – never for them. Throwing caution to the wind, there is something of a false exuberance and an underlying smugness about many middle-ranking officers, concerning the Corps' future. They fail to recognize that we live in a rapidly changing world, which will affect their lives and that of the Corps they so faithfully serve. Survival will entail more than saying, 'Make way, here come the Marines.'

Royal Marines have fought gallantly in all parts of the globe for over 300 years. Being part soldier, part sailor, Marines have also distinguished themselves on the high seas and in the air. They campaigned in the Anglo-Dutch Wars of 1665, the French Revolutionary Wars and the Napoleonic Wars. There were Marines in the Boxer Uprising, the Opium Wars and the Crimea. Marines operated a Camel Company in Egypt in 1885. Along Britain's coast, during the Second World War, they helped to construct sea defences. They took part in the Malta convoys, the Dieppe Raid, the landings at Salerno, on Sicily and the Normandy coast. There was a Royal Marines Major who commanded a guerrilla operation behind the Japanese lines in Malaya. Off the French coast, in the dead of night, silent shadowy figures slipped away in two-man canoes launched from a submarine. The world came to know them as 'The Cockleshell Heroes'. Churchill's personal bodyguard was made up entirely of Marines. As the Empire faded, they helped to quell the bush wars in Aden, Cyprus, Palestine and Malaya. And as the twentieth century declines, Royal Marines are still at war, boarding suspect ships in the Gulf and fighting terrorism in Northern Ireland. Over the years, ten members of the Corps have been awarded the Victoria Cross.

As Britons, there is a mite of the *Boys Own* element in all of us. Marine commandos evoke the 'glory factor'; the green beret reminds us all of clandestine operations, guile and cunning. What man is not seduced by dare-devilry, blackened faces and macho imagery? All men must dream and have their fantasies. Were the Corps structured to accept female entrants, surprisingly few women have so far expressed a wish to join; no doubt dissuaded by the stifling brand of chauvinism many have experienced while serving with the Marines. There is more than ample evidence for saying that, like the majority of British society, and the military establishment in particular, the Corps is a sexist institution.

As in many of Britain's military institutions, the NCOs are the powerhouse of the Corps, the mainspring of the commando spirit. They know the short cuts, and how to wangle and get things done. Humour and generosity are their stock-in-trade. While many would deny it, the officer corps are still sensitive to criticism following the Prince Edward saga. By no means élitist, they are recruited mainly from middle-class families. Though the public schools are represented, the incestuous nature of that system has thankfully failed to control the Corps, with by far the greater proportion of potential officers coming from the lesser-known schools in the land.

It is said that the officer corps possesses an unacceptable touch of arrogance – no matter, somewhere there is a touch of arrogance in all of us. Along with excellence and invincibility this makes up a military trilogy. Though no longer wielding the influence of past decades, the officers' influence is nevertheless considerable, reaching into the Royal family, politics, commerce and industry. In their defence of the Corps, they still pack a punch.

This book is a documentary about the Royal Marines, seen in the light of the fast pace of a changing world. Since my accreditation to the Corps I have tried to peel away the layers of a military society with my Leica cameras and tape recorder. Being an outsider, at times it has not been an easy task, for Marines are by nature suspicious and clannish. They prefer to get on with the job, rather than talk about it. From the outset I was given complete freedom to wander throughout the Corps, photographing and talking with whomever I wished. Marines have their secrets and they guard them well, therefore it has not been my purpose to pry into areas that affect our national security. My aim is to present a human documentary, similar to my account of the French Foreign Legion. In the same tradition, except in a few cases, I have maintained throughout the principle of anonymity. Many of the conversations I had with members of the Corps were on the understanding that I would not betray their trust. My book is neither historical journal nor exposé, but contemporary reportage about the Royal Marine Commandos. Access to the Corps was given without any obligation on my part to show them the completed work before publication.

As I criss-crossed the world photographing and speaking with hundreds of Marines I resolved to produce the finest possible picture documentary on the Royal Marines in the final years of the twentieth century. I know that I have told an objective story. It remains for my readers to pass judgement.

PART 1

IRELAND

THE MARINES
AT WAR

BELFAST
AUGUST 1989

Northern Ireland duty is an arduous task. Monotony and boredom are as much the enemy as the IRA terrorist. With limited recreational facilities, many Marines work a 14-hour day, some even longer. There are continuous day and night patrols together with members of the Royal Ulster Constabulary (RUC) around the infamous areas of West Belfast, where the sniper and bomber lie in wait for the security forces.

Even when the sun shines, Belfast is a depressing place. Here the Gaelic spirit is but an illusion, for everywhere there is a haunting sadness that envelops the place. For all that, surely there must be joy and compassion somewhere in this beleaguered city? Instinctively, the stranger feels the hostility, the anger and the unrelenting hatred that pervade every street and alleyway. Even the children are affected, for where is their laughter and child-like innocence? Such is the contagion of Belfast that many who live here do not see it this way, for years of violence have dulled their sensitivities, while for others it has all become a weary irrelevance. The simple truth is, that the people of Ulster have tranquilized their feelings.

The 'Troubles', as the locals so delicately describe their violent malady, are confined to the ghettos of West Belfast and the Republican countryside around South Armagh and Crossmaglen. In the prosperous middle-class areas of the city, around Malone and Belmond, the plastic bullet, sniper and the 'drogue' grenade, the accoutrements of death and violence, belong to a lurid other world. Without a doubt, the middle classes here can lead a cosy and comfortable life, immune as they are from the high mortgages and poll tax of the mainland. True, throughout much of the Northern Ireland countryside and the greater part of Belfast, the security services, in their converted olive-green and grey Land Rovers, are a rare sight.

The Tourist Board, and similar promotional machinery, will remind the visitor in their glossy brochures that within a few miles of scarred and deprived Belfast the 'Troubles' hardly exist.

In reality, Belfast is a war zone and it would be foolish to pretend otherwise. Nor is the conflict confined to the city alone, or to a few Republican enclaves in the countryside. It is an Irish problem to be solved by all the peoples of Ireland on both sides of the border. As the violence has matured, the security forces have become more street-wise: deserted streets, open windows and protruding wires are signs of danger, which they treat with suspicion. Around-the-clock airborne surveillance – the all-seeing eye – collects valuable intelligence, monitoring the movements of known suspects.

Good intelligence is essential in the fight against terrorism. Marines spend hours memorizing the faces of known members of the IRA. Knowing the 'players', as they are called, is an essential ingredient of intelligence gathering. With high-powered optics and cameras, Marine observers in their observation post (OP) in the Divis Flats, Belfast, play a vital part in the operation.

In this revolutionary society some of those who live on the edge of the terrorist ghettos – the police and members of the Ulster Defence Regiment (UDR) – for the most part Protestants, are inevitably soft targets for the gunmen and the bombers. Like the migrant British troops, who live and work in armed cantonments, their life is one of meticulous precaution: homes become fortresses sprouting electronic gadgets to safeguard them and their families; each time they are used, cars are searched for bombs; and there is a constant awareness not to regulate their lives in any way.

Twenty years have passed since that fatal night on 14 August 1969 when a bullet ended the life of 24-year-old John Gallagh on the violent streets of Armagh. Since then Ulster has been in a state of near civil war. During that time more than 2,760 soldiers, police officers and civilians have been murdered by one or other of the terrorist organizations. Shrouded in despair, various shades of British and Irish politicians have attempted unsuccessfully to pacify the population with fanciful ideas and solutions, the most recent being the Anglo-Irish Agreement of 1985. Sadly, none has been successful.

As the endless murderous rituals continue, Governments blunder on. Pragmatism and containment, it would appear, are the only epitaph to this sorrowful dilemma.

A confusion of obstacles is sown along the road leading to the entrance of the old North Howard Street Mill – concrete blocks and barriers that prevent a direct approach. High up, cameras scan the area for unwelcome intruders, but somehow they seem oddly out of place prying into the tottering remains of the surrounding landscape. With its controlled approach, high walls, observation towers and electronic cameras with zoom lenses, the old mill is today a well-defended bunker. On the flagpole by the gate the company flag hangs motionless, waiting for the evening breeze or a current of air from the deserted alley. It is a Legion fortress overlooking the traditional alien terrain.

Constant vigilance and the professional expertise of colleagues are the Marine's only safeguards while patrolling West Belfast. The deserted street and the open window could be a warning of an impending terrorist attack from a well-concealed gunman.

The control room monitors all Marine and police patrols within its area. Operating around the clock, control-room personnel plot the movement of their patrols and, in an emergency, deploy all the necessary forces to deal with the incident.

Although the accommodation in the old mill is spartan, the Marines make the best of their surroundings. They are an adaptable lot, and have the resourcefulness to make their temporary 'home' bright and comfortable.

As any Marine will tell you, their role in Northern Ireland is a thankless task. They are there, we are reminded, to support the civil law enforcement agencies; the police and the courts.

Since the first British soldier was shot dead in February 1971, Britain's role, and consequently its military involvement, has become increasingly complex. When our troops first moved on to the streets of Belfast in 1969 they were, for a short time, enthusiastically welcomed by the Catholic community. Lieutenant-General Sir Ian Freeland, the General Officer Commanding in the Province at the time, foresaw a 10-year stay by the military; he believed then that he was being unnecessarily pessimistic. Now, twenty years on, his prophetic insight can be seen as being sadly restrained.

One of the earliest lessons that the military had to come to terms with was a revision of infantry tactics in urban areas. Their enemies were terrorists who had no respect for the Geneva Convention. At that time the military was issued with the self-loading rifle (SLR), a most unsuitable weapon for this kind of guerrilla warfare. All Marines are now issued with the lightweight SA 80. With its reduced length and telescopic sight, it is a far better weapon for the streets of Belfast. Marksmanship also needed improving. Firing from the conventional positions at a fixed target was antiquated thinking, which should have ended with Gordon and Kitchener, for rarely did this enemy allow you the luxury of the classic prone position. Statistics revealed that 75 per cent of shooting incidents occurred at night at ranges of less than 150 metres, most of the time at moving targets.

Certain military strategists, when discussing Ulster, will claim that our forces have gained a great deal of tactical experience from the conflict. However, such a theory is challenged by others, who argue that it has been a costly experience, both in lives and expenditure. Duty in the area is also disruptive to other major exercises. When Marines are committed to Ulster duty, a commando can be tied down on emergency duties for a period of nine months or more (the present 4^1/$_2$- month term is to be extended to six months). This includes special training prior to going there, and a period of readjustment on return to the mainland. As well as giving several generations of officers and NCOs experience of commanding men in combat, it is generally accepted that the Northern Ireland experience had certain advantages when it came to retaking the Falklands; the battles for Port Stanley and Goose Green were in part won in Belfast and Londonderry. Our Marines are the finest counter-terrorist force in the world, but a degree of scepticism exists nowadays within the Corps regarding the tactical benefits of Northern Ireland.

Most of the British Forces in Northern Ireland are frustrated by the shenanigans of all the politicians. Left to their own devices, Royal Marine Commandos could clean up all the terrorist activities in Ulster within a few weeks, but the Westminster Government is acutely aware of international criticism, especially from the Irish-American lobby. So, instead of placing Belfast under marshal law, and hunting down the terrorists with ruthless determination, our politicians prefer to juggle the system, oscillating between the doctrine of appeasement and containment.

North Howard Street Mill lies between the Falls Road and Shankill Road in West Belfast. It is the headquarters of 'K' Company 42 Commando Royal Marines for their 4^1/$_2$-month tour of duty in Belfast. At one time, no doubt, the clatter of looms could be heard throughout the 4-storeyed building. That was years ago. The fragrant smell of tweed and linen has long since disappeared. The old, ramshackle mill with its soot-stained brick is a sober, windowless building and, apart from a few slatted openings here and there, the autumn sunlight rarely enters. Protecting the occupants from the prying eyes of the sniper, concrete breeze blocks now replace windows, adding a further touch of grimness to its ageing façade. All around is waste ground, supporting the dilapidated remains of buildings – their innards collapsing and rotting. It is a no man's land.

Life behind the walls and electronic defences might well be claustrophobic, if you gave it too much thought. Activities around the mill by its occupants are discouraged. Areas are screened, so that the prying eyes of terrorist sympathizers are prevented from obtaining car numbers or from photographing personnel engaged in undercover activities. It is difficult to tell how many Marines live here; even if it were possible, it would be unwise to say. Inside are airless rooms and constricting walls.

Built to withstand bullet or grenade attack, green and grey Land Rovers are the familiar vehicle of the security forces throughout Northern Ireland. Visored helmets and bullet-proof jackets are worn at all times while on patrol.

Hatred and confrontation are written across the walls of West Belfast. Rarely do the inhabitants speak to the security forces. Attempts made by the Marines to communicate with the local population will be rejected and their presence is frequently met with abuse and overt hostility.

'What I miss most,' says one of the attractive Wrens working there, 'is good fresh air – you just don't get it in here.' Life under such imposed hibernation has been compared to living in a giant underground bunker. Everything, from the control centre to the sleeping accommodation, is enveloped in a greenish hue from the naked overhead striplighting. Living is cramped for everyone. In some cases there can be as many as a dozen Marines to a room.

Fatigue can be as dangerous as a sniper's bullet. A wrong decision made when tired or under stress could be fatal. Everyone is living under stress out here, where an 18-hour day is not unusual. Commanding 'K' Company is a Captain. By all accounts he should be in his mid-thirties, but it is difficult to tell. The office lighting casts sombre green shadows everywhere. Normally his face is tanned from wind and sun. Tonight it has a pallor, it is taut and tired. The military frame, usually erect, is weary. He wears a green T-shirt with a commando motif, combat trousers and boots.

'How many hours have you been on duty?' I ask him.

'I started at eight o'clock this morning and will finish at two a.m. – an eighteen-hour day.'

My next question does not surprise him. Others have, no doubt, asked him the same thing.

'You're making important decisions. How can you do it after eighteen hours on duty?'

'We are put under pressure in controlled conditions in training to deal with these kind of problems,' he tells me. 'If I felt tired, I would stand down and put myself to bed for an hour after lunch. It's a question of adjustment. You learn to manage and conserve your energy.'

The Captain goes on to explain that his principal role is to support the Royal Ulster Constabulary (RUC). Routine patrols, house searches, even the delivery of a summons for some trivial offence could mean an escort of eight or ten Marines.

Looking up at his operations map on the wall, the Captain outlines his 'patch'. He is adjacent to the city centre in West Belfast: to the north is the Protestant Shankill area; to the south the largely Republican stronghold of the Lower Falls, Beechmount and Whiterock.

'It's about six square kilometres, perhaps a little less. My Marines patrol around the clock. It means some eleven hundred man-hours of patrolling every twenty-four hours.'

He knows his patch well. How many hours, I wonder, has he prowled around this area, with his Marines, getting to know every nook and cranny? He knows all the likely ambush spots, and where they have recently unearthed bombs – what the military call improvised explosive devices (IEDs).

'This is our greatest problem.' He holds up a common piece of flex, similar to a household telephone cable. 'You can buy it anywhere. At the end of it could be half to twenty-five pounds of Semtex and a simple firing mechanism. The firing point could be a hundred metres away.'

Every so often, usually after a terrorist has been

Life within the mill never stops, for patrols are coming and going around the clock, and in the control room patrol movements are constantly monitored. The whereabouts of a suspect are logged. An abandoned vehicle, reported stolen, is sighted in an alley off the Falls Road. The bomb squad is sent to investigate. The emergency detail is alerted. It is hard to believe that the mill and its surroundings are an integral part of the United Kingdom, and as British as Eastbourne or Blackpool.

shot by the security forces, some politician or other implies that the police and the British troops have a deliberate shoot-to-kill policy. I ask the Captain about his rules of engagement. He is quite specific.

'When a Marine is shot at by a terrorist, clearly he is aiming to kill the Marine. The Marine will return fire in an attempt to kill the terrorist. Our Marines will fire the minimum number of rounds to achieve their aim when they are sure that they can identify the firing point. There is no justification for indiscriminate firing if the firing point cannot be established.'

The Captain talks about an operation planned for the early hours of the next morning.

'We are supporting the RUC in several house searches. A patrol will bring you out at daybreak.' Cocooned in the pale-green interior of the operations room, he continues with his plans for the pre-dawn raid.

Dawn is greeted by a rare, almost unholy sound – the clatter of the all-seeing helicopter, and the Angelus from the nearby church. Surely only in Belfast could you awake to such discordant notes? Breakfast is a slurped coffee and soggy brown toast. Two hours after dawn and the sky is still grey and overcast, threatening rain. Near Cupar Street, on the Falls Road, the Marines have set up a safe area from which to monitor the operation. Like a western wagon train under attack, three armoured personnel vehicles (APVs) are clustered against a nearby wall, forming a small defensive compound. Flack-jacketed Marines wearing perspex-visored helmets train their SA 80s on nearby buildings. Cryptic messages crackle over personal radios. The Captain and a Major speak in monosyllables, while studying a heavily pencilled map of the area. Two hundred metres down the Falls Road a group of Marines armed with electronic bomb-sweeping equipment carefully scrutinizes cars, removes manhole covers and, with the aid of portable ladders, peers on top of walls. Crouching in doorways, others scan the area through the telescopic sights of their SA 80s. All around life continues. Old ladies collect their pensions, breweries unload beer and the local postman delivers mail. The inhabitants of the Falls Road pay scant attention to the Marines, for this is part of their daily life. They have seen it all before.

The Captain suggests that I join one of his patrols that are about to enter the rabbit warren of streets and alleyways to the north of the Falls Road. An energetic young Lieutenant is detailed to look after me. He knows the area well and gives a lively commentary on our surroundings. For the unsuspecting, this is a dangerous area of West Belfast. It is strongly Republican: graffitied walls spell out the hatred, murals with their crude revolutionary symbols inform the stranger that this is a combat zone and Irish Republican Army (IRA) territory. As we swiftly cross the deserted intersection, I catch a glimpse of youthful faces under visored helmets. Apart from the Corporal, the Marines' average age can be no more than twenty-one. There appear to be about eight or ten Marines in the patrol; it is difficult to determine their number exactly as they roll and slither from doorway to doorway. They are agile and nimble, but at the same time they move with care and caution. Their eyes are everywhere. Every so often they scan the street and houses through their powerful telescopic sights, searching for the tell-tale glint of the sniper's rifle. Occasionally a Marine will attempt to pass the time of day with a child or ageing granny. Rarely do they receive a reply; only the cold stare of hate.

Every Marine has been highly trained for the streets of Belfast, his marksmanship finely honed. Two stout elastic bands secure a small map of the area to the butt of his weapon. He can read the danger signs in streets and alleys. He has spent weeks studying the faces of known 'players' (terrorists and their sympathizers), and he knows who they are in his area and reports their movements by radio and at patrol debriefings. On his return, everything is remembered, and reported: newly abandoned cars, heaps of rubbish, freshly repaired roads, even disturbed and loose bricks on the sides of houses.

There is one street that is neater, a little tidier than the rest. Windows are polished, some freshly painted. A grey-haired lady in a black cardigan and skirt is watching our activities with interest, so I take the opportunity to talk to her. Nearby the Marines of 'K' Company, their backs flattened to the wall, keep watch on both entrances to the street. As the morning has brightened, I begin with the weather.

'It's a lovely day.'

'It is indeed,' she replies in a lilting brogue that sounds more like Dingle Bay than Belfast.

'You have a lovely little house. Have you lived here long?'

'Nineteen years or more. I live here with my brother.'

It appears that the row of houses was probably built about 1840. When I enquire about the value of the local property, she has no reservations about telling me the value of her home. Glancing inside she says, 'I should think that this house is worth

During a routine bomb search operation, a member of the public is questioned by Marines.

about fifteen thousand pounds.'

I detect that she is beginning to feel uneasy at my presence, so I depart. It is strange, but she has made no reference to the Marines; why we are there, or what we are doing. For her, like everyone else in Belfast, it is all perfectly normal. Younger generations have known nothing else.

Nearby, a specialist team of police and military is completing a search of a suspect's home. Marines have cordoned off the area in a street of modern, brick-built semi-detached homes. It could be any nondescript neighbourhood in Barnsley or Brighton, with its tidy front gardens, porches and brass door knockers. At one end of the street a small group of onlookers is curious to know what is happening. Aproned housewives peer from behind half-opened doors. Unseen hands gently slide aside front-room curtains to reveal inquisitive faces. Oblivious to all this, the milkman trundles on his way on his daily round along the near-deserted street. The Warrant Officer shouts to one of the Marines to get behind a garden wall, to improve his cover.

A passerby, well built and in his mid-thirties, is stopped by two of the Marines. Something has made them suspicious. I see that the Marine across

the road has shifted his aim to cover the suspect. Three automatic weapons now point at him. Unperturbed, the others maintain their watch along both sides of the street. One of the Marines had seen something suspicious in the man's left-hand pocket. The object turns out to be a two-way radio transmitter. It is well known that the IRA try to monitor police and military frequencies, and terrorist sympathizers also maintain a steady flow of information to their local IRA cell by means of inexpensive portable transmitters such as this one. Is this man passing information to an unseen terrorist concerning our activities? Rapid checks are made on the suspect's identity over the Marines' radio. Within a few minutes the tension has eased. Our passerby has satisfied the Marines that he is not involved in anything mischievous. He slouches off in the direction of the onlookers at the bottom of the street, the offending transmitter aerial still protruding from his left-hand pocket.

The search team appears from inside the suspect house. Nothing has been found. We quickly slide into the armoured vehicles, and a rapid check ensures that everyone is accounted for. We speed off as quickly as we arrived. The small band of onlookers withdraw into their homes. For the

With armoured patrol vehicles forming a secure area, officers direct a bomb search operation in West Belfast.

second time that morning, unseen hands shuffle front-room curtains and the faces disappear from the windows.

If there's one landmark in Belfast that is better known by the security forces than any other, it is the notorious Divis Flats. The flats are dingy and graffiti-ridden, and are occupied on each floor by members of the Catholic community. The Divis are familiar to generations of British servicemen, for they are as famous as Kelly's Cellars on Bank Street, or the Albert Clock Tower at the end of the High Street. From the top of the flats the whole of Belfast spreads itself before you. Eastwards lies the River Lagan and the heart of the city. City Hall can be clearly seen on Donegal Square, as well as the Albert Bridge. Northwards is the Shanklin Road, while to the south is the Lower Falls. It is hardly a breathtaking view, but from the Divis everything can be seen, making it an ideal observation post (OP) for the military. On top of the flats are two large Portacabins: one is the operations and observation room; the other, living quarters.

Throughout the Province there are several OPs similar to the Divis Flats. They provide excellent surveillance points into some of the most important areas of IRA activity. Then there are hidden or covert OPs set up in deserted houses or in some innocent-looking junkyard or car lot. Surveillance information from Divis and other OPs, along with information from informer networks, is fed into the intelligence computers for analysis by the RUC and MI5. It is a well-known fact that 90 per cent of the 'players' are known to the security services. In a recent shooting incident, a member of the security forces knew his assailant, though he had not seen him fire the weapon. Later, while on patrol, he came face to face with the man on the street, each knowing who had fired the near-fatal shot. Such is the paradox of Belfast.

The daily battle between the security forces and the terrorists is a cat-and-mouse game. It is a secret war of spooks and informers. Good intelligence is the key to any operational success, but there are times when high-grade intelligence can also present a dilemma for the security men. Information can be so good that it could compromise a well-placed mole, alerting the IRA to an informant in their midst.

Our two armoured personnel vehicles draw up

close to the Divis Flats. Six young Marines, armed with SA 80s, fan out and take cover. My escort tells me to wait until our vehicle has reversed closer to the entrance. A lanky young Marine has appeared at the door to the flats holding a cocked 9mm Browning automatic pistol in his right hand.

'Let's not hang about, get over there.'

My escort pushes me out of the APV towards the Marine with the pistol. Entering and leaving the OP requires elaborate security precautions. Weapons are cocked and a series of radio checks ensures maximum security, as we enter and leave the lift that takes us to the top floor of the 18-storey building. Ladders and a trapdoor take us on to the roof and to the entrance to the OP.

Inside the entrance, someone with a wry sense of humour has erected the following notice:

For sale – luxury flat with two toilets, showers and washrooms, living room and galley. Own launderette, fitness aids, large pantry with upright freezer, loads of food, fully furnished, central heating, own generator, low-cost rent, Cougar radios, TV and video plus your own helipad, east and west wings so that you can see the sun rise and set or enjoy the scenery on the spacious balcony. Yours free!

This is a top-secret area; part of a network that resembles Bernie Sampson's secret and seedy twilight world of intelligence and counter-espionage. On the walls are photographs of known and wanted 'players'. Young Marines peer through powerful optical equipment logging the movements of a specific 'target' in the street below. There are cameras with lenses as long as your arm. Television monitors glow in a darkened corner, while a telex machine purrs out a silent message. A young Marine speaks quietly on a miniature radio while observing his 'target' through a snub-nosed telescope.

'If it's busy in there, the time can fly by,' says the Corporal on duty. 'If it's dead and you have to observe more closely to find a "target", it can be strenuous. Yes, it's very satisfying, especially the "TR" [Terrorist Recognition] side. It's a challenge to find a new face, find out who he is and what he does. It gives you a sense of achievement as you pick them up. We've had an improvement in the sightings since we started.' He mentions the figures to illustrate his point.

He does not underestimate the enemy. 'The top players are good, but there are a lot of hangers-on. I suppose it's the social position it brings them.' He continues, 'You meet them [the players] in the street every day, and you have to speak to them as normal people, without letting on too much how much you know about them. You could know a lot more about them than you let on.'

Marines are, on occasions, accused of having a quirky sense of humour. On one of the doors is a small notice, which reads:

I like this job so much, I'd do it for nothing – unfortunately they know that!

Beneath is a small Union Jack.

Ask any Marine about Northern Ireland duty and he will tell you that for most of the time life is a tedious routine, for apart from the few extra pounds in his pay packet, it has few redeeming features. It is a no-glory war with a faceless psychopathic enemy. Days are interminably long. There is no social life, and you are fettered to the cavernous interior of a military compound during your off-duty hours. You live in a time warp, where weekends are something you imagined a long time ago and weeks blend into months without you knowing it. Life becomes a monotonous merry-go-round of patrols, television, beer in the NAAFI, a workout in the gym and, some time during the tour, the greatly anticipated four days' R and R (rest and recreation). In the end your sole reward is the funereal green and purple campaign ribbon, proclaiming to the world that you are a veteran of the fight for the 'bloody bog'. Allow yourself to become complacent, even for an instant, and the consequences can be fatal.

It was professional instinct, courage and outstanding leadership that saved one patrol from certain death on the streets of West Belfast.

It was one of those rare balmy June nights, and all around Belfast the polling stations were about to close. It was the time of the European elections. For Corporal Brent Woods, a cheerful, earnest young NCO with twelve years' Marine service, for him and his colleagues, apart from being election night, it was no different from any other. The patrol was looking forward to returning to Springfield Road police station, where they knew hot coffee awaited them. Donegal Road lies in a notorious Republican area near the Beechmount and Turflodge estates. As they moved along it, Woods felt instinctively uneasy about the derelict house on his right, and he shouted for the patrol to move into the centre of the road to avoid it. He sensed there was something wrong; there were the open windows and the unlit street lights. But it was too late. The bomb exploded.

In the rich, warm brogue of his native Nottinghamshire he recalls, 'It felt as if the world was caving in on me. I was lifted up and carried across the road for about forty feet.' His words are slow and hesitating, spoken with a slight tremor, even though it is weeks after the near-fatal night. 'I picked myself up knowing we had an explosion contact.'

It was only when he heard the cries of his patrol that he knew they were alive. Without fear for himself, or the injuries he might have sustained, he quickly assessed his casualties. Two of his Marines were seriously injured and the police accompanying him were also in a grave condition. Perhaps there were other bombs waiting to go off, as it is not unknown for terrorists to plant a second device in an attempt to take out the follow-up teams. Within seconds he was going through the drill they had rehearsed so often. Immediately he gave a contact report over the portable radio. It was detailed and precise. In cool, clear language he gave his position and the casualty details. He requested police, ambulance, bomb disposal team and tracker dogs, and gave a 'steer' for the follow-up team, indicating the likely location of the firing point. It was only after he had assured himself that the members of his patrol were on their way to hospital that he realized

that he was also injured. His left side was numb, there was an agonizing pain around his neck and a deafening ringing in his ears.

'I was only doing my job,' he says, as he recalls the fateful night. 'I still wake up at nights dreaming it was me they were after, but I know that it could have been anybody.'

Like many war veterans, Brent Woods has a feeling of guilt. He blames himself for his injured comrades.

'It should have been me in front of the patrol, but instead, I put myself as the third man.' He speaks hesitatingly about his future. 'I don't know if I shall stay in the Marines. This explosion was a little bit too close to home. In the Falklands I never came close to dying. I don't mind dying for Queen and country, but it must be an enemy I can see. It must be an enemy I can fight. One good thing, we all came through it. It was the professionalism of the team that got us through the incident. We spread out and it saved us. My wife doesn't want another Northern Ireland. She has the same sort of feelings as me. This place is not worth putting your life on the line for.'

After two decades, the killing fields of Northern Ireland are as ripe as ever. Perhaps it is now time to review our policy in Northern Ireland.

Throughout West Belfast, sectarianism is underlined by the political and religious mural.

THE PADRE

Within the military pecking order it is traditionally recognized that the padre's role transcends the usual hierarchical military rituals, with all its clubland gallantries and social ramifications. To claim an effective ministry the padre must be able to move smoothly from the cliquish officer groups to the comfy, outspoken sanctum of the NCOs' mess, and on to the affable, yet more ascetic, Marines' quarters. He must, at the same time, endeavour to be all things to all men, for the very nature of his work makes him a man of trust and an intermediary.

As one padre remarked, 'I see my place very much among the trainers as well as the trainees here at Lympstone. From the newest recruit to the Commandant, I hope I am of some use; whether it is out of experience or a fresh mind, or someone standing slightly outside of the system who can look in on something.'

As the Marines have something of a dual personality – part Navy, part Army – it is Navy padres that for the most part minister to the spiritual needs of the Corps. Padres, along with everyone else in the military training business, have seen attitudes change; all of them agree that a dozen or more years ago people would blindly follow the system, whereas today everyone is far more questioning and critical of ineptness. Like most churchmen, Marine padres are aware that it is essential to identify with their flock; stuffy hide-bound clericalism would achieve little in the Corps and serve only to alienate the average 'Bootneck' (Marine). So, to get the feeling of being one of the family, wherever it is physically possible, padres who find themselves with the Marines have a go at the All Arms Commando Course and try for the green beret.

One very fit-looking Marine padre describes his lifestyle before joining the Corps. 'I was ordained in Bristol in the late 1960s, and spent five years there ministering to a pretty rough council estate; an interesting place with some super people. It was pretty red-blooded, with hatchet-wielding wives and drunks. Then I moved to Suffolk and opened a brand new church, which was a patch of mud when I first arrived, then was left wondering what on earth I was going to do, because I felt that anything else wouldn't really challenge me. So I wrote to the Army, Navy and Air Force all in the same day, and the Navy replied first. Though you wouldn't believe it now, I had long hair, blue suede shoes, and was very trendy in those days.' He continues, smiling, 'I went off to see the Chaplain of the Fleet, who took one look at me and obviously it crossed his mind that possibly I could serve with the Royal Marines!'

To be frank, Marines, like most military institutions, do not readily embrace religion; instead, they view it from a distance, preferring to savour it and participate in its offerings when the occasion demands. The service padre's role is modified to meet the needs of his congregation, while the sacraments of the Church may be dispensed when required. The greatest needs of those around him are those of friend, counsellor and social worker; in general, an earthly intercessor. It is equally important for a padre to be available to discuss the thorny problems of the 'just war' or AIDS as it is to prepare a Marine for confirmation or marriage.

Speaking about Church life within the Corps, the padre goes on to say, 'I work on the principle that if you don't invite people in, then they don't know what you are doing. I never refuse child baptisms, even though I know that people don't necessarily come to church. I allow it to happen, but there are ways of allowing it to happen. If you go around and hit Marines over the head with a Bible, you may as well pack your bags and go; they are much happier to know somebody, and through knowing somebody start to get the response.'

The transition from civilian life involves a host of adjustments for the young 'Nod' (recruit), in many cases involving leaving behind a girlfriend. Some of the youngsters, before beginning their training, even embark upon the first stages of matrimony, which in most cases is bound to fail.

The padre elaborates, 'I have an enormous amount of guys who have girlfriend problems; the thing that flattens them is the "Dear John" letter. The girl at home, who maybe he's been in love with for two or three years, suddenly says she can't cope, very often because he is here and can't get home – so the girl goes on to pastures new, and the poor guy is left here. What I say is, life is worth living, it's odds on that he has another sixty years of life. You must put things in perspective. It is all wrong to think that because young lads are becoming Marines, or

Royal Marine officers receive Holy Communion from a Navy chaplain on board HMS *Intrepid* prior to taking part in an exercise off Sicily.

hoping to, they have left all emotion behind. I find it quite the opposite. Marines as a whole are well known for being as soft as butter inside. Anyone wants to raise money for anything – the Marines will do it. All we have to say is that there is a sick child somewhere, and they will do whatever they can to help. At a recent carol service here at Lympstone, five hundred pounds was raised for the Russian earthquake disaster.'

The padre pauses for a moment, running his fingers through his thinning, sandy-coloured hair.

'One of the lads was having the usual girlfriend problems – it was quite serious – and I managed to get him home. A little while later I saw him looking down in the mouth and found that he had spent so much going home that he didn't have fifty pence to do his *dhobi* [laundry]. I have a little contingency fund, so I gave him some money, and said, "For goodness sake if you are short of money say so, because I can provide it." He went away, and with a little help managed to survive the month till pay day. I saw him in the corridor out there and went out and said, "Congratulations, green beret, thrilled to bits. . ." Just as he left he had something in his hand, and he said, "Here you are", and it was the money I had lent him. I had forgotten all about it. He insisted that I must take it. "You helped me out and I've come to repay you," he said quietly.'

THE WOMEN AND THE CORPS

While the Marines see themselves as being profoundly superior to any other part of the British military system, although far from being élitist or stuffy, they still retain the inherent outmoded attitudes of London's clubland and die-hard public schools in their attitude towards women. Therefore it is hardly surprising that most women regard the Corps as an introverted chauvinistic world; a world in which they are allowed to perambulate only when the need arises. Even then, it is by invitation. Most women marrying Marines know what to expect – long periods of separation, managing the family unit on their own, creating a near independent lifestyle with the occasional jaunt to the mess for the Summer Ball, an outing with the kids to the annual Open Day and the seasonal trip to the Christmas pantomime. They appreciate that it is all part and parcel of the idiosyncratic military persona.

With long periods of separation inevitable, the divorce rate among the Marines is high. Higher than the national average. Some are on their third marriage; this is one of the reasons why Marines and NCOs leave the Corps after five or six years' service. Young Marines see the hazards caused by long separations from their wives and sweethearts, and so depart from the Corps for a more stable lifestyle. Many NCOs have similar feelings. For some, their time is spent shuttling between duty in Northern Ireland and winter exercises in Norway. It is a lifestyle that strains relationships. Loved ones can change beyond recognition. Fathers become strangers in their own homes.

At home the Marine is little different from the thousands of other Britons across the land: he takes the kids to school, potters in the garden, natters with the neighbour over the garden wall, and no doubt helps to prepare the occasional meal. He is loving, kind and generous, remembers the children's birthdays but usually forgets his wedding anniversary. He will jog most mornings and keep extremely fit. Apart from the uniforms in the cupboard and the occasional pile of military equipment on the bedroom floor, when he's home, life is more or less the same as in most homes around the nation.

Needless to say, away from the confines of domesticity another view is gleaned from the other women in his life – those with whom he works.

Wrens are proud of their professional abilities within the naval service. A small number of them work with the Royal Marines in various capacities, from photographer to general administrator. They volunteer for Marine duty and have definite opinions about the 'Royals'. Perhaps Marines may not realize it, but Wrens are pretty shrewd in their assessment of them.

As one Wren remarks, 'In some ways we know them better than their wives and girlfriends. After all, we work beside them every day.'

There is both praise and indignation from the women who come into contact with the Marines.

'At first I felt like a monkey in a cage, they were always watching us. After a while it died down,' was the comment of one young Wren who had served with the Marines in Northern Ireland. Asked to expand on her experiences, she says, 'They're not used to working with women. They try to embarrass you all the time.'

How does a young lady keep her femininity surrounded by strapping Marines hungry for female company?

'You don't out there,' she replies. 'You're not as feminine as you are normally. Your conversation goes down a step. If you came in all dolled up to the nines, then they'd class you as somebody different. Out there, you've got to be one of the lads.'

In circumstances where the Wrens share the same bathroom, toilet and sauna facilities as the men, modesty is quickly overcome by everyone.

'You've not got to be embarrassed,' emphasizes one of the young Wrens. 'Normally you wouldn't dream of walking into a shower with the lads in there. When we go back to our normal establishment you just wouldn't knock on the blokes' toilet and walk in. Out there you just have to do it.'

There is an underlying feeling of disappointment among some of the Wrens who work alongside Marines. Some feel like appendages, devoid of all professional abilities. Marine officers are seen as lacking finesse, manners and gentility, when compared to their naval counterparts.

Such is the experience of a Wren officer who has also served in Northern Ireland – we'll call her Jane. Jane has been a Wren officer for five years; now an administrator, she is attractive, articulate and a graduate. How does she regard the Marines?

'If I am going to be frank, when I came back from Ireland I was very disappointed, mainly because my expectations were high before I joined the Marines. Wren officers are very well trained in administration, and we know there are right ways of doing things. To go into a situation where the administration is severely lacking – things were being done on a day-to-day basis – that is what disappointed me. I like to get things right and I found it difficult to make the system work. I suppose with Royal Marines, their main concern is being military men, leading men in the field, so little attention is given to day-to-day administration.'

Jane is equally outspoken about mess life.

'I found the Royal Marine officer rather young and immature towards guest females in the mess. The joking that goes on when females are gone. I love to say to them sometimes, "I wish your wife or girlfriend could hear you talking like this."'

There was a marked difference between naval and Marine officers in their attitude towards women.

'The Royal Navy officer,' she goes on, 'treats you as an equal. He recognizes that you are an officer and a female officer, as well as a professional doing a job. I think that a Marine officer has difficulty in accepting the fact that you are a woman with the same rank as him. When you are in the mess, naval officers will stand when you walk into a room, open a door, or stand up as you arrive in their company. They recognize that you are a lady as well as an officer. After all,' Jane continues, 'women in the Armed Forces are not advocating that they wish to be mean, green, fighting machines. But we are saying, recognize us for what we do well.'

Living and working with Marines is perhaps best summed up by the remark of another Wren officer. 'Wrens either love working with Marines or they hate and loathe it, and can't wait to get out. Many who have served with the Marines go back to them again and again if they can possibly wangle it.' Why? 'They're treated very well, a rarity.' A good husband catch? She smiles and continues, 'Women tend to marry the men they work with. No, I don't think it's about getting husbands, I really don't. It's quite nice being surrounded by attractive men.'

Despite enjoying working with Marines, there are things she resents.

'I dislike Miss Globe and Laurel [the Corps pin-up]. It's nothing to do with her being a pretty girl with lovely legs. It puts women in their place – women are there to be attractive, decorative and to make extremely light conversation.'

She reflects for a moment.

'Why do I like working with them? Despite their inherent chauvinism, once you can prove you can do a reasonable job, and you're not a stupid, empty-headed woman, which is how they tend to categorize you, they give you credit for any work you can do. To work with Marines you have to have a well-developed sense of humour and a very tough hide, because you get a lot of teasing. Marines tend to appreciate people who give as much as they get. Not all girls like that.'

There is little doubt that attitudes within the Corps will change, and that women will be admitted into the Marines within the next few years. Certainly before the end of the decade. It is simply a question of time, and the sooner the better. After all, women are at long last being allowed to serve at sea for extended periods on Her Majesty's ships. While it is not intended that women (Wrens) serving in the Navy should be in the 'firing line', should a naval ship be caught up in a local conflict, then Wrens will be involved in front-line action. Surely this is no different from the current situation of women members of the Armed Forces serving in Northern Ireland?

For some inexplicable reason there is a squeamishness within the defence 'squirearchy' about allowing women to serve in the front line. It is all part of the puritan ethic which believes that the male is the dominant force within the family unit.

It is an illogical concept, for women are both fighters and survivors. Women command ships, sail the world single-handed, fly multi-million-pound airliners around the globe and manage international companies. Some have been propelled into space, while others have climbed the world's highest peaks. During the Second World War women were parachuted into occupied France as couriers and radio operators. They endured Gestapo interrogation and torture. Others died in the death camps rather than betray their country. Single-handed, women ferried fighters and bombers across the Atlantic. On the Russian front, Soviet women fought beside their male comrades through savage winters, from Stalingrad to Berlin. Women make formidable guerrilla fighters. In Palestine they fought in the Hagannah, as they did in Vietnam against the Americans. There are women who are terrorists, operating on the streets of Belfast and wherever else their so-called 'cause' may take them.

Men are mistaken in believing that women are fragile creatures. After all, Britain has a remarkable Monarch, and had, for more than eleven years, a formidable woman as Prime Minister.

PART 2

TRAINING
SOME ARE CHOSEN
BUT FEW SUCCEED

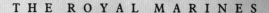

As any Marine will tell you, the green beret commando course at Lympstone is only the beginning of his training. Throughout the year a young Marine can be sent on a variety of courses to perfect his skills as a commando. Each year Royal Marines fine-tune their mountain training and field craft in the bleak and hostile terrain of northern Scotland.

THE RECRUITING OFFICE

'When I joined, my pay was ten or eleven shillings a week, now a young lad takes home a hundred pounds.'

Recruiting Officer, Brighton, Sussex

Queen's Road, Brighton on Britain's south coast is hardly a prime example of the Regency architecture of which the town is rightly proud; tired rather than seedy, the road has a miscellaneous collection of shops and offices, with Victorian façades in various stages of disrepair. Within a bugle call of the newly renovated station with its lattice ironwork trim, and opposite the staid, balconied Queen's Head Tavern, is the local Armed Forces Recruiting Office. In the window, forlorn without its Whitehall spit and polish, is a Lifeguard's ceremonial dress uniform. Inside there are easy chairs and all the usual persuasive material to entice the nation's youth to consider accepting the Queen's shilling. Military recruiters are hard-pressed. Few young men will even consider the Queen's offering, let alone accept it. It would appear that these days the bugler's call is blown in vain!

There is one exception. The Royal Marines, it seems, have something that still appeals to Britain's young men. Perhaps it is the added nefarious title of commando that strikes a note of high adventure and derring-do. Whatever it is, the Marines are attracting all they need, regardless of their equally high resignation rate – nearly 3,000 Marines and officers during the current year (1989/90).

'Barring the drop-outs, our Potential Officer Courses [POC] are full for the next eighteen months. Mind you, if someone turned up with impeccable qualifications, and I thought he would fit into the family, we would make room for him,' says one of the Corps' young officers involved in the selection process.

Could he tell when a young man stepped through the door if he had the potential to become a leader of men in the world's finest fighting force?

'You get a feeling about a guy after chatting with him for a while. All the time I am asking myself, does he have the right motivation? Without the motivation all the brawn and the education won't help. In the end it always comes down to: would I have this man in my troop, or want him alongside me when the going got tough?'

Marine selection is an expensive business. An aspirant to the nation's commando force is sent on a three-day Potential Recruits Course (PRC) at the Corps' training establishment at Lympstone, in Devon, which can cost the taxpayer an average of £400 for each would-be Marine. Regardless of this, the Marines feel that it is money well invested, for the filter process saves a great deal of time and anguish for those who would never complete the course. For the Corps, it saves further expense in training, were they to find the recruit lacking the necessary qualities at a much later stage. As it is, there are a great many who fail. From a recent batch of twenty-eight would-be Marines, sent from the south coast on a PRC, only twenty-two arrived at the Commando Training Centre. Of those, fourteen finished their three days' trial period, and eleven were accepted for training. According to Marine statistics, roughly 50 per cent complete the 36-week training period, which means that of the original fourteen perhaps six may get to wear that coveted green beret.

'We don't paint a rosy picture,' continued a Marine Warrant Officer in the Brighton Recruiting Office. 'I tell the lads who come in here that they could be on patrol in Belfast within a few weeks of completing their training, and they will be spending a lot of time digging snow holes in northern Norway, but it doesn't seem to put them off.'

As for qualities, he continues, 'We are looking for a sound education from a comprehensive school, a man who has a keen love of outdoor activities – camping, mountain climbing, canoeing, that sort of thing – plus a good work record. A well-motivated lad who is quick on the uptake.'

Although for the moment the Marines are riding high in the military careers stakes and do not have a recruiting problem, like the rest of Britain's Armed Forces, the high numbers leaving the Corps are causing grave concern among the Marines' top brass. Marines will tell you that the days of the 'good drafts' (postings), as they call them, are gone, and the annual trek to the Norwegian snows, coupled with the dangers of Northern Ireland duty, is not the way most of them wish to spend the remainder of their lives.

LYMPSTONE
COMMANDO TRAINING CENTRE

'The Royal Marines are a very close-knit, close-welded, highly motivated killing machine, which is there to pursue the nation's defence interests.'

A former Royal Marine officer

It is one of those soft mizzling February mornings that makes the Devon countryside glow; although spring is near, a wintery harshness still surrounds the landscape. On the platform of what must surely be Britain's smallest railway halt, a Royal Marine NCO, pace-stick tucked neatly underarm, strides purposefully up and down the miniature platform. He casts a glance at the slate-coloured sky, murmurs to himself as he walks, the gentle rain making small, rolling pools on his prized, mirrored boots.

The railway halt – it could never be called a station – is a military establishment; only recruits, Marines and groups of civilian employees alight here. Lympstone is an enchanting place, though few recruits notice its beauty when they first arrive. Across the one-track railway are the glistening mud flats of the Exe estuary. A faint breeze wafts the tangy salt air inland. At low tide only a narrow channel of water tumbles into Lyme Bay. There was a time when the area was ostentatiously referred to as the Devon Riviera, coined, no doubt, by ageing matrons retiring here from Purley Way, Cheam and Sutton. Familiar Devon towns are all around: Exmouth, Dawlish, Salterton and, although not on the same scale, the 1,000-year-old village of Venn Ottery. To the north-west, as forbidding as ever, lies remote and perilous Dartmoor: mysterious, sombre and beguiling.

As the 4-carriage train approaches along the single track from Exeter, the NCO carefully adjusts his tie, smoothes the jacket of his lovat-green uniform, then passes a finger across a fair, well-trimmed moustache. He carefully eyes each passenger as they alight on to the lilliputian platform. Though a nondescript lot, these are no ordinary passengers, and it is no ordinary place they have come to. The dozen or so young men who have alighted at the appropriately named 'Commando Halt' have travelled at Her Majesty's expense from all corners of the British Isles in search of something that means more to them than anything else in their lives. Some will never attain it, while others will bust gut and limb to wear it. In money terms, it is inexpensive – worth six or seven pounds, no more. To the wearer it is a crown of gold, a cherished garland, his degree for life. It is the green beret of the Royal Marine Commandos.

All recruits spend their first fourteen days in the induction block. It is a halfway house, a buffer between the cosy civilian world they are about to leave and the stark military one that awaits them. Like the postulant monk, the young recruit is entering a strange and, at times, bewildering environment. These days 'Marineization' is accomplished by means of gentle firmness and understanding: Lympstone has devised a muted approach towards the young men. Unlike some military institutions, the divestment of personality will be gradual. Before accepting the Queen's shilling, every recruit will have spent a three-day trial period at Lympstone in order to savour this strange sea-soldier environment. To maintain a tolerable resignation rate – already far too high, according to some critics – young men seeking to enlist in the Marines are sent, all expenses paid, on this Potential Recruits Course. It is a time for getting the toe wet, a taster of the real thing. For this period young men can become make-believe commandos, wear military dress, eat in the recruits' galley, tumble through part of the assault course, experience a brief 'yomp' and be lectured on the merits of the Corps. Like prospective lovers on their first candlelit supper, each is eyeing the other for their strengths and weaknesses. Some never return, others are told to spruce up and try again, the remainder will be invited to join the long, hard course for the green beret.

It is surprising just how much care and concern are taken in receiving the recruits. For instance, there is a noticeable absence of overbearing NCOs bellowing instructions. No banshee-wailing commands. Nor are there any barbaric rituals, or fiendish 'old-timers' with a never-ending stream of barrack-room jokes and horror stories. Such inveterate military customs are, for the most part, now a thing of the past. To allay the almighty rush for the window bedspace, all spaces have been allocated

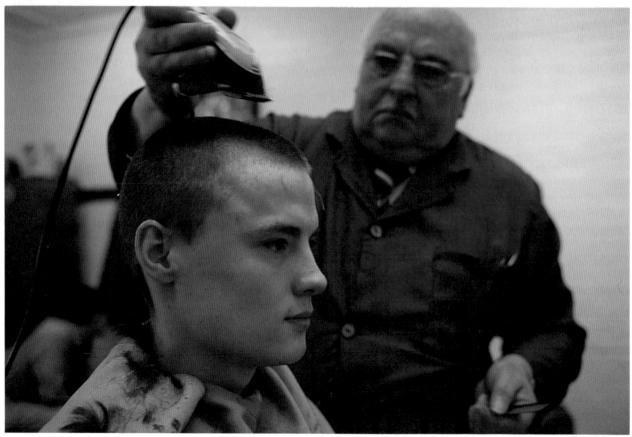

before the recruits' arrival. That evening, in a dimly lit, tiered lecture room, still dressed in their civilian clothes, the fifty-three members of Troop 571 are instructed by a hawk-eyed Colour Sergeant on how to sit to attention.

'When the Captain comes into the room, you straighten the back, look ahead, *don't fidget*, arms straight down at your sides, and when the officer greets you, you *will reply*, "Good evening, Sir." Is that understood?'

In attempted military unison everyone replies, 'Yes, Colour Sergeant.'

A bellowing 'Attention!' echoes around the room as the Captain walks in. All the desks quiver slightly. Chins are thrust forward, arms straightened at the side. Each senses that atmosphere is all-important for the Captain. Immaculately uniformed in green lovats, green beret at exactly the right angle, he wears a small cluster of ribbons headed by the MBE. There is little doubt in the recruits' minds that this lean-faced man of indeterminable age is all-Marine. For the next ten minutes or so he speaks of their obligations to the Corps, and the Corps' obligations to them. It is a get-up-and-go pep talk that he has obviously given many times before. It is forthright without being gung-ho.

They are going to be trained to be the finest infantry soldiers in the world, he reminds them. They are going to be taught to kill, and come back and kill again. For most of them the prospect of killing or being killed has never entered their heads. There is a long silence. It is effective, for the Captain likes long silences, to emphasize his point. His piercing eyes sweep each row in turn.

'Now, does anyone want out before taking the oath of allegiance?' he enquires. Silence – no one has moved; not a shuffle or a cough. 'Stand up, take the Bible in your right hand and repeat after me, stating your name clearly.'

Ten minutes later Her Majesty's Royal Marines have increased their compliment by fifty-three. Troop 571 has completed its first official act. Tomorrow will be day one in a new life, which, for some, will take them to the far ends of the earth.

Creating the right atmosphere – setting the tone – is a vital ingredient in the Lympstone training cycle. Granted, in recent years there has been an exceptional transformation in all the Armed Forces' training programmes; however, nowhere is this more evident than at Lympstone. Yesteryear's Marines will not hesitate to tell you that in their day training was ruthless, at times almost brutal. It was a malevolent society, invoking submission and humiliation, where NCOs ruled in feudal-like fashion. Thankfully, such thuggery has long since disappeared from the Marines. Young recruits now experience a training programme not unlike that of athletes being groomed for Olympic stardom. Everywhere there is a delicate blend of nurtured discipline. Instructors – at times there is a ratio of one to five for a particular training period – will encourage and push, never bully or ridicule.

'Come on, Smith, you can do it, lad – swing that leg, up and over, hang on, don't let it bloody beat you.' This is a familiar encouraging plea heard from instructors trying to help a recruit across a particularly difficult water obstacle. He falls in. His penance: ten push-ups. As he races to change into dry clothes the instructor shouts, faintly sarcastically, 'And we'll have to do it again, won't we, Smith?'

Remorsefully the recruit replies, 'Yes, Sergeant.'

In conversation, the Captain responsible for the recruits' early weeks of training, who has 'Marined' the hard way – through the ranks – elaborates on his welcoming set piece. Rightly the Corps believed that with thirty-five years of service he projected the appropriate spirit to be in charge of their fledgeling commandos.

'I try to light the fires of enthusiasm that will drive them through thirty weeks of training – pointers that will get them over the bad times. I aim to give them confidence and continue their education as citizens.' He has a paternal warmth. Like a solicitor briefing a client embarking on litigation, he speaks in slow, measured phrases. He continues, 'I try to allay their fears about their instructor/officer relationship. Here, young men can ask questions without their heads being bitten off.'

Meanwhile, each member of Troop 571 has been issued with several hundred pounds' worth of kit, including shoes at £25 per pair. Each has had the regulation snooker-ball haircut, for which he has to pay £2. He has also had a pay advance, which, for the Marines' forefathers, would have been a king's ransom – £50 – for such personal requirements as soap, cleaning materials and the all-important black Kiwi polish. The majority of

Recruits – known as 'Nods' to the instructors – arrive at the Royal Marines' Training Centre, Lympstone, in a variety of dress and with mixed feelings. From an average troop strength of forty, they are told that only half of them will complete the course. Within a few days their civilian identity will have diminished. With shaven heads and wearing military attire, from now on they will endure an exhausting 14-hour day.

the young men of Troop 571 are northern lads from the bleak, economically deprived areas of New-castle, Carlisle, Glasgow and Liverpool. Five are from the West Country, with the most northerly coming from Inverness and the most southerly from Plymouth. Fresh-faced and eager, for some it is their first experience away from home. Their ages range from sixteen to twenty-four years.

Academically the troop is reported to be above average. Five have the necessary qualifications for a commission. Twenty-one come from what is con-sidered to be disturbed backgrounds, while more than half the troop have fathers or relatives who once served in HM Forces. In the clinical, non-committal wordage of military reports, Troop 571 is a 'sound and well-balanced course'. That some of the recruits have embarked on the first step to matrimony by becoming engaged before savouring their new careers could, it is thought, cause 'set-tling difficulties'. An insight into their social classes is seen from some of their fathers' occupations: one is a plant operator, another a works foreman, one a building contractor and another a former Lieu-tenant-Colonel who now works for a computer company. All come from what the British euphe-mistically call the 'upwardly mobile'.

It is late evening on the second day. In the induction block the 24-hour-old recruits are franti-cally ironing and polishing piles of newly issued kit. It is interesting to note how uniformity is envelop-ing them. All have shorn, bristly skulls. All are wearing their newly issued gymwear: white shorts, green tops and chic, expensive trainers. Two of

their instructors, impassive and weary from twelve hours of nursemaiding their charges, move from group to group answering questions on how to do this, or that. Already several recruits have started cleaning their hulking black parade boots. One of the expressionless instructors decides it is time to demonstrate the old soldiers' technique of boot-cleaning.

'Right, gather round, lads. I'll show you how it's done. You *can't* get a good shine without first taking out the wrinkles. *This is done with a hot iron.*' With a touch of dull humour he speaks firmly and slowly, scanning each face in turn to make sure they understand. '*Then*, it's hours and hours of spit and polish. You make little circles like this.' Eager ado-lescent faces watch every move and hang on to every word.

There is an incomparable tedium about clean-ing a hefty pair of military boots. That intelligent young men should be expected to while away end-less hours embellishing their footwear with the ritzy shine of a pair of dance pumps is, to say the least, bewildering. For dress and ceremonial pur-poses, the United States Marine Corps is issued with patent-leather footwear. Surely our military budget would not be drastically affected if our recruits were issued with something similar?

In the meantime, relationships are beginning to form within the troop. NCOs have carefully explained the old Marine principle of the 'buddy system'. 'To survive you have to work together as a team!' chorus the instructors.

Some of the recruits are already using Marine-

Maintaining a high standard of physical fitness is essential for the Royal Marine Commando. Dawn work-outs on a remote beach in northern Scotland are all part of their routine training.

speak. By now they will have realized that all recruits are called 'Nods', Marines are 'Bootnecks' and that they will go to the 'heads' instead of the toilet. Each eats 'scran' (food) in the 'galley' and after a 16-hour-day will be all too ready to collapse in their 'grots' (rooms).

With the surfeit of films produced by Hollywood on the brutality of war and the military in general, the average person would be forgiven for thinking that commando training is vicious and relentlessly brutal. These days this is not the Royal Marines' style of doing things. Nevertheless, busting your gut for thirty weeks to earn your green beret is not easily forgotten. With great skill, the foundations of the embryonic Marine life are laid with minute care. Like groups of student nurses, the young 'nods' are taught to make their beds. Sheets are perfectly creased, pillows fluffed and counterpanes draped in the appropriate fashion. Contents of wardrobes have an order: civvies here, uniforms there, toiletries here, writing materials and books there. For this diverse collection of young hopefuls, such disciplined orderliness will not come easily.

In the cool morning sunlight a one-time Marine, a Second World War old-timer, reminisces on how Lympstone was in his day.

'Reunions bring back old memories.' Deep shadows cast by the early morning light reveal the contours of a weathered, ageing face. In his time Lympstone was a collection of wooden 'billets', heated by wood-burning stoves, the kind you see today in chic barn conversions. Although he lives only a short distance away, it has been forty or more years since he was last at Lympstone.

'It's all changed since my day. None of this was here.' He sweeps his stick across the campus-style buildings surrounded by trees and neatly groomed shrubs. 'In my day the "galley" was over there by the guard room. My pay was seven and sixpence a week. When I married, it was a couple of bob more. Mind you, I could get a pint in the NAAFI for, let me see now, ninepence, I think. Don't know how we managed on the money – but we did. These young 'uns don't know what it's all about.'

Things have indeed changed. Defaulting recruits no longer slop whitewash on everything in sight. The carbolic smells that once pervaded all military establishments have been replaced by the lavender and lemon odours of the aerosol. Nowadays, contract gardeners mow the lawns on brightly coloured motor-mowers. Others prune heavily scented rose bushes. In the spirit of Enterprise Britain, both officers' and Sergeants' messes will soon be managed by private companies. Even now the Sergeants' mess has all the atmosphere of a well-run country golf club – there are separate rooms for snooker and television, two bars, plush leatherette sofas and armchairs. Above hang shimmering ballroom chandeliers. Each morning the crisp daily papers are neatly arranged for all to read. All are there, from *The Times* to the tabloid *Sun*. There are menus on the tables. Tea is at four, with delicious Heinz sandwich spread, Marmite and a variety of meat pastes. For the early arrivals there will be gooey cream cakes. The old veteran would

After attending a three-day Potential Recruits Course, where the aspiring Marine is given a taste of what it's like to be a commando, the Corps then decides upon his suitability. At Lympstone, the Commando Training Centre, no time is lost in shedding the recruit's civilian identity. During the evening of his first day, he takes the oath to the Monarch and the Corps. At an indoctrination lecture before taking the oath, he is made aware that the months ahead will be hard and fearsome, and that for a variety of reasons many will be rejected during the course of training. Some things in the Marines never change. Boots and cap peaks must always shine like mirrors.

never have believed that Marines could live like this!

For all the changes and improvements brought about in the Corps in recent years, there is one area of change that is highly contentious. It concerns discipline and how it is administered. Senior NCOs are lamenting the lack of discipline and the lowering of standards to qualify for the green beret. As one instructor commented, 'Today we are getting a different kind of recruit. He is better educated, and more than likely comes from a middle-class family. Twelve to fifteen years ago, you would be getting a poorly educated young man, possibly with the arse hanging out of his trousers, but who would respond immediately to what the instructing staff would say. Today, youngsters question orders.'

Time and again instructors confided that some recruits, whom they personally had recommended for back-trooping or discharge, are being retained.

'It's the old numbers game,' one instructor said. 'Regardless of standards, a certain number of the troop have to pass, otherwise it looks bad on the returns. In my troop at the moment there are half a dozen blokes at least who should be kicked up the backside and out the front gate. It's not fair on the rest of the troop if the deadbeats are allowed to get away with it.'

In one of the instructors' offices there are several disgruntled training staff. One of them is so despondent that he says he is 'jacking it in' and requesting a transfer back to a commando. For others it is even more drastic: they are leaving the Corps. It is not a question of disloyalty; they love the Corps and all it stands for. As far as they are concerned, they are not getting the support of their superiors.

'A walk around the back of the drill shed and a thump around the ear, that's what I got,' says one of them. 'But you can't do that today. They're too well educated. They go and complain to their padre or Member of Parliament.'

This is not an isolated bunch of discontented Marine instructors. Similar comments can be heard elsewhere. On the other hand, instructors are not advocating the mind-bending vindictive methods of some foreign armies.

One of the Corps' senior Warrant Officers gives his view. 'Our young recruit is a very high-calibre Marine. He is aware of all his rights. People have

more rights than they used to. With the old system there were a lot of injustices. There was a lot of bullying. I do not believe we should humiliate anyone. However, if a man is run up and down a hill until he drops for being insubordinate, that is different.'

Senior officers are adamant that there is no lowering of standards. As far as they are concerned, there is nothing wrong with the system. After all, they remind you, their training and the quality of their men helped Britain to regain the Falklands. Most are content to let things continue as they are, with occasional adjustments to the tiller to ensure that nothing stagnates. As one senior officer says, 'It is difficult to make changes quickly, even if you want to. It is important that what we do here is evolutionary rather than revolutionary. Changes must be progressive.'

Not surprisingly, for some trainees, Lympstone is a shock to the system. Five-thirty a.m. starts and a 16-hour-day for little more than one pound an hour is not their idea of commando life. Their imagined Rambo lifestyle is short-lived, and they slope off through the front gate within the first few weeks.

Whatever misgivings NCOs have about their charges, they are perhaps being unduly critical. While on patrol with these young men in the sniper- and bomb-ridden streets of West Belfast, I witnessed their professional expertise at a very personal level. Several were in charge of my safety. I firmly believe that I could not have been protected by a finer body of men anywhere in the world. Their vigilance was unending, without being oppressive. Their good-natured ribald humour never ceased, even at the end of a 16-hour-day.

Surrounding Lympstone is the lush, green Devon countryside; in autumn and winter it can be shrouded in swirling mist, as if viewed through etched glass. Devon folk are mainly farmers and fishermen, toughened by searing Atlantic winds and rugged, open terrain. Also, this is tourist country. The busy Exeter road passes by Lympstone's gate. Throughout the summer, endless streams of screeching holiday traffic weave and meander their way to the sea. As if to emphasize the nature of Britain's Marines, everything about Lympstone is quiet and unobtrusive. Were it not for the sentry at the gate and the discreet signs at the side of the road – unnoticed by most passersby – you might believe that the puritanical stone buildings were a rural polytechnic or prosperous agricultural college.

The Commando Training Centre Royal Marines, better known in military circles as CTCRM, is a collection of modern buff-coloured buildings built on rolling farmland that unfolds down to the sea. Architecturally there is little to commend them, for they are neither harmonious nor pleasing to the eye. However, without a doubt Lympstone's facilities are a vast improvement on the draught-ridden Victorian citadels of other Marine establishments at Eastney, Plymouth or Deal.

It is unlikely that anyone in the Western military community would deny that Lympstone is the epicentre of commando training. Within the special Forces' fraternity, the Royal Marine Commando is envied for his dedicated, no-nonsense professionalism. Even the immodest United States Marine Corps concedes that the 'Royals' are something special – a breed apart. On the surface Lympstone has a quiet, rustic charm. Do not be fooled: beneath the surface there is a war-like effervescence. Territorially it has none of the vast acreages of Sandhurst or the US Marines' Parris Island in South Carolina. Rightly, however, the Marines believe that they have some of the world's finest natural training areas in their own back yard: Dartmoor and Exmoor, with their fickle weather conditions, can savage a man within hours, if he is unprepared and untrained.

Lympstone resembles a small military village. Like most villages it is self-contained and gossipy, with all the social undulations of any small community. Overseeing the training and the day-to-day life is a full Colonel assisted by a staff of 100 officers, 376 NCOs, a handful of Wrens and 128 civilians. At any time throughout the year there could be 500 recruits in training, together with a batch of thirty to forty trainee officers. As you might expect, a great deal of kinetic energy is expended at Lympstone. Vigorous, exercise-ridden endless days and nights produce hungry men with enormous appetites. Annually Marine recruits and their trainers drink more than 129,000 pints of milk, devour 38,000 loaves, 31,000 pounds of carrots, 6,963 kilos of cheese and open 7,614 cans of beans.

The 'village' has its own church, barber's shop, several tailors, a superb gymnasium with a 14,000-square-foot sprung floor, a near Olympic-size heated swimming pool, a sports shop, bank and the ubiquitous NAAFI, without which no British military institution would be complete.

Military communities have changed. They have an almost human atmosphere these days. Shrill commands and the once predictable bawling of the drill instructor are, if not a thing of the past, certainly more muted. Obviously there is a purposeful air about Lympstone. Even when not with their troop, recruits march around with arms swinging at shoulder height, heads erect and eyes staring beyond the horizon. Everyone is neatly dressed and well polished, without being over-sanitized or peacock-strutting. Marines are aware that warfare has become more technical. Brawn and 'bull' were for the colonial wars. Intelligence and resourcefulness are the natural commodities of Britain's contemporary commandos.

Roughly speaking, a young Marine commando's training is divided into three phases. First come his two weeks in the induction centre, where he is taught the rudiments of military life – how to wash and iron clothing, personal hygiene and general tidiness. Nothing is left to chance. 'You wash beneath the armpits and around your crotch,' an instructor reminds them.

By mastering simple routines early on, the recruit will find life in the barracks, and later at sea, more comfortable. Instructors will be constantly hovering in the background, gently enforcing routine, order and discipline. Already the sifting process has begun. At the induction centre the recruit can leave at any time. Similarly, the Corps may decide that he is unsuitable. By the third week he has been moved into permanent recruits' quarters. Veterans would no doubt envy him, recalling the cold, airless, cell-like accommodation of their day. Nowadays, it is six to a room, with personal wardrobes, sheets and coloured bedspreads. A recruit's 30-week training is divided into phases: a 15-week pre-commando toughening-up period, followed by an intensive 15-week commando training period.

According to one of the training team, Troop 517 is still 'rough'. 'It's pretty depressing to see them,' he says. 'They lack any kind of motivation. They haven't caught on to the idea of the buddy system yet.'

Will they eventually?

The idea that the troop is below standard obviously worries him. 'They'd better start pulling their fingers out soon, or we have a problem.'

By week eight the troop has lost four of its number. Forty-nine remain. More advanced troops have higher losses. For one reason or another, some have lost twenty or more recruits.

To strengthen the muscles, physical training instructors take trainees on to the mud flats of the River Exe.

'You could see it coming,' one young recruit commented, referring to his former mate, who has departed.

Speaking about another of their troop who has left, one says, 'When he got a bollocking, he would take it to heart. It was on his mind.'

On the training, another remarks, 'In the first few weeks we were bored. I didn't like it at all – now it's what we expected. I am surprised how much we have learnt.'

As the weeks pass, the instructing team increases the pressure – exercises throughout the night; map-reading across alien terrain in soaking clothes, blinded by rain and numb from the freezing cold of Dartmoor. One of the instructors is relating some of the hazards in the bar one night. 'Exmoor is the worst. Being so close to the Atlantic, you get the full force of the weather coming off the sea. It's the barbed-wire fences. If you're not careful, you can get your bollocks ripped off.'

Recruits will be expected to live off the land. To survive they will need to snare or fish for their food. At night they will sleep in crevasses or bivvies. As if this were not enough, all the time they must remain operational in case they are ambushed by the watchful 'enemy' – their instructors.

Few, if any, of the recruits will have had any previous experience of living off the land. Most of them will be 'townies', who will have been raised among the urban sprawl of our large towns and cities. Marine life will drastically change their living habits. Their lives are now timetabled from dawn till dusk. Their 16-hour day begins at 0600 hours with a bugler playing Reveille. A good close shave and a shower are mandatory, otherwise they could find themselves being chastised by one of the instructing staff on the morning parade. It is bedlam in the washrooms, as everyone jostles for a washing space with mirror, and a shower. A hurried breakfast before 0700 hours, when they must draw their weapons from the armoury and be on parade by 0800 hours. Meanwhile they have had to make their beds, make sure their lockers are tidy, and assist each other in cleaning their quarters. An hour-long parade and drill is followed by exercises and lectures – there could be as many as three throughout the morning. The one-hour lunch period is mainly spent preparing for the afternoon programme, which is equally frantic, alternating between the gymnasium, firing practice on the range, and a lecture on a future night exercise. The evening meal – Marines always call it supper – is at

1754 hours. Until 'lights out' at 2230 our novice commandos will be cleaning equipment for the following day. Their only relaxation might be a beer and a natter in the NAAFI, followed by a phone call to parents or girlfriends.

Most military units have their own assault course. They are fiendish devices ostensibly designed to strengthen and invigorate an infantry recruit's training. Whatever the regiment or unit, be it at Pirbright or Parris Island (USMC), they will tell you theirs is the most devilish. The Marines have devised three assault courses which, together with other gruelling tests of endurance, form the basis of their green beret examination into the Royal Marine Commandos. Every morning you will see muscular physical-training instructors bellowing a litany of exhortations to their young charges.

'Go on, lad, give it stick!' shouts one instructor in a broad Midlands accent. Crimson-faced and lathered in sweat, the hapless youngster swings his way across a series of parallel bars.

For those who are practised in these things, some of the obstacles could be regarded as comparatively easy. There are low and medium-sized walls, simple-looking jumps, and such like. Others, involving scrambling nets and ropes strung across water tanks, where Marines are expected to dangle and recover, are nothing but awesome. As if the obstacles are not fearsome enough, recruits, after a carefully monitored tune-up period, hurl themselves through the various obstacle courses in full battle order – carrying thirty pounds of equipment plus their weapon.

Anyone will tell you that the toughest of the three Marine tests is the endurance course.

'It's a right ball-breaker,' one instructor says.

The course has been planned around the neighbouring moorland. Here the land is coarse, tufted grass, boggy and steep. To succeed you have to have the stamina of an ox and the sure-footedness of a mountain goat. There is flooded moorland to ford, water-filled pipes to negotiate on your belly, and a 4-mile run for 'home' – all to be completed within seventy-three minutes. It does not end here. On arrival, each recruit is expected to fire accurately on the 25-metre range.

Prior to being awarded his green beret, the young recruit must pass a series of commando tests. Failure can mean relegation to another troop for further training. The Marine is trained to be an athlete who can 'yomp' for days in full battle order, as was demonstrated during the Falklands conflict. One test involves 'yomping' nine miles in ninety minutes.

Every military institution takes pride in the fiendishness of its assault course. Marines believe theirs to be the most ingenious and demanding of all, for they have added a further element – the Tarzan Course – which recruits must complete in five minutes. Taken consecutively, the assault course and the Tarzan Course must be completed in thirteen minutes, all in full battle order.

The mountainous regions of northern Scotland are an ideal training ground for abseiling (*right*). Royal Marines hold the world record height for abseiling.

Over the years, crusty drill instructors have maintained their familiar parade-ground banter. For them the parade square is sacred ground. They demand perfection and get it. Meanwhile recruits nearing completion of their training are fitted for their lovat green uniforms in which they will receive their green berets (*far right*), watched by their admiring families. Proud parents, Lieutenant and Mrs Cameron March, record the day their son, Marine Duncan March, received his green beret (*main picture*).

It is Friday, 13 October 1989. There is a chilly wind blowing up from the sea as the King's Squad marches on to the Lympstone parade ground. Mums and dads, brothers and sisters, all wearing their Sunday best, have come from all parts of the kingdom to see their boy pass out as a Marine commando and be presented with his green beret. Huddled together on benches, the families seem hardly to notice the chill autumn air. Tartan rugs cover exposed limbs. Woolly scarves are wound around necks. The Royal Marine Band plays all the old familiar tunes: 'Life on the Ocean Wave' and Sousa marches. There are the usual predictable speeches, meant to be uplifting and patriotic, which few hear, let alone care about. Later there are family photographs beside the commando memorial, and frothy pints to be consumed with Uncle Bill and Cousin Fred. It's a day everyone will remember for the rest of their lives. The day their lad received his green beret. Tomorrow the erstwhile recruits will be on leave, re-living their memories, and some enjoying mum's cherry cake. Next month they will be in a commando unit. Next year it could be Belfast or the frozen wastes of Norway. Troop 571 has passed out. Of the original fifty-three who arrived more than six months previously, only twenty-nine survived the course.

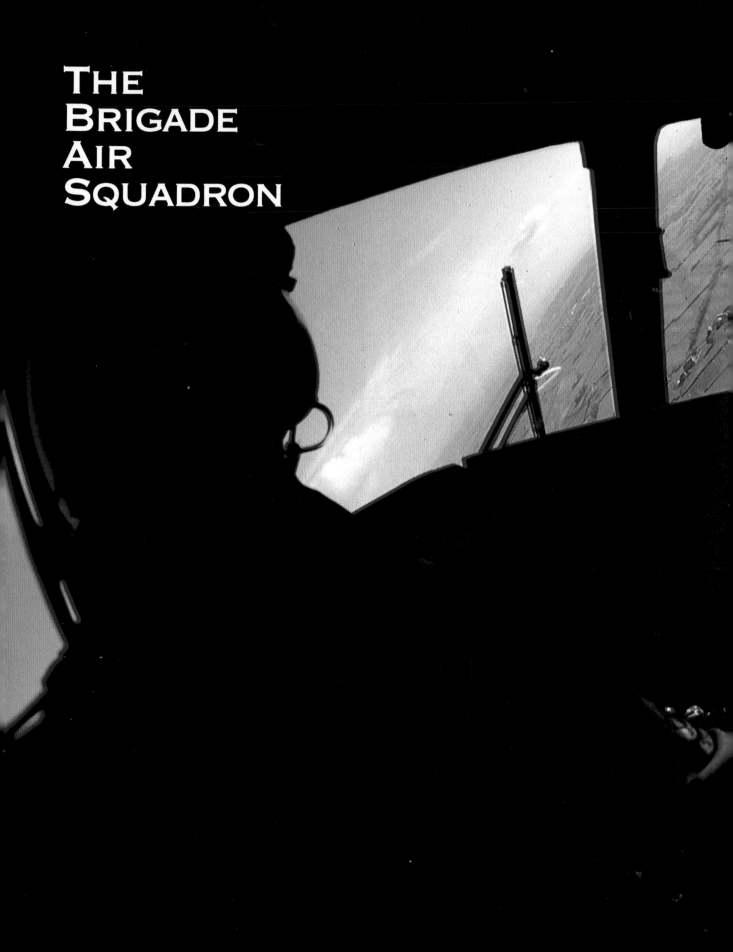

THE
BRIGADE
AIR
SQUADRON

After a detailed weather briefing two pilots, a Sergeant and a Corporal, dressed in drab olive-green flight suits and carrying well-travelled Royal Air Force flight bags, saunter out to one of the Lynx helicopters parked on a remote airstrip at Saillagouse in southern France; within minutes they will be airborne on a routine mountain flying exercise. They carry out their pre-flight drills: the Corporal carefully inspects the airframe and rotors, chatting with the Marine ground-handler on the way round; meanwhile the Sergeant neatly folds his green beret, places it in his flight bag and puts on the regulation space-age flight helmet with its dark-green sun visor. Removing the black cotton protective cover from the visor, he looks at the distant Pyrenees, already snow-capped, for winter is fast approaching, and ponders on the strength of the down-draughts along some of the valleys through which they plan to fly. Together the pilots go through the pre-flight check list: radio frequencies set, all instrumentation functioning, temperatures and pressure in the green; and with the high-pitched whine of the engines, the airframe shudders, as they take one last look all round. The ground-handler indicates that all is clear, and the Corporal engages the rotor clutch as the Sergeant brings the aircraft into a hover. With a steep nose-down attitude they gather airspeed and begin climbing to their operational altitude. On some of the far-off peaks it has begun to snow.

In northern Norway another helicopter of 3 Commando Brigade Air Squadron, this time commanded by a Major with a Corporal as his co-pilot navigator, is assisting in a local conservation exercise. They are flying in an area to the north of Trondheim, carrying two forest rangers who are tracking the movement of moose with the aid of miniature radio transmitters, which have been fitted to the animals. All the moose are counted and their location marked on maps by the Norwegian rangers.

At Middle Wallop in Hampshire, the home of the Army Air Corps, another two Marine pilots, this time a Corporal and a Lieutenant, along with their Marine ground-handler, are representing the Corps in the British Open Helicopter Championships where, against world-class competition, they gain eighth place.

Most people are surprised to learn that the Royal Marines have their own air squadron; Marine air power is, after all, supposed to be the preserve of the United States Marines, and the idea of the 'Royals' having any kind of air power is received by many with a degree of sceptical disbelief.

As far as the pilots of the Brigade Air Squadron (BAS) are concerned, they would like to be less dependent on the RAF. As one of their pilots says, 'Compared to the Yanks we're only playing at the flying business. What we are badly in need of is a first-class attack helicopter. Come to that, there's no reason why we shouldn't have our own Harrier Squadron either.'

Mention improved air cover for our Marines to any of the Corps chiefs and they will become evasive and tetchy. As far as they are concerned, improving their air power is not on their list of priorities. For the time being, at least, the RAF will supply their extra needs; more important, the Generals will tell you, are new assault ships and a much-needed commando carrier.

Britain has had Marine helicopter pilots for more than twenty years now: BAS came into being in 1968, not in Britain, as one might expect, but at Dieppe Barracks, Sembawang, in Singapore; in those days the Marines had fourteen Sioux AH Mk 1 helicopters. Today the squadron has six Lynx and nine Gazelles committed to three flights – two Gazelle flights and one Lynx.

For a little-known part of the Marine Corps, the squadron has a fine pedigree: its pilots and helicopters have flown on missions worldwide, from Sarawak and the South Atlantic to terrorist-ridden Ulster. Awards within the squadron include one Military Cross, two Distinguished Flying Crosses, One Distinguished Flying Medal, one Air Force Cross and two British Empire medals. Nine members of the squadron have been Mentioned in Dispatches.

During the Falklands campaign, the whole squadron went to the South Atlantic and was used mainly to evacuate the wounded and to ferry ammunition and supplies. Brigadier Thompson, their Commander at the time, says of the Brigade Air Squadron, 'Without light helicopters and their gallant aircrew, many young men alive today would be dead, many of our attacks would have foundered

Britain's Marines have had their own helicopter squadron for more than twenty years. Trained by the Army Air Corps, the Brigade Air Squadron operates Lynx and Gazelle helicopters from the Royal Navy base at Yeovilton, in Somerset. Though ground-handling and refuelling are carried out by Marines, all the squadron's helicopters are serviced by the Army. With defence cuts to Britain's Armed Forces imminent, many Marine helicopter pilots are now contemplating a flying career in the private sector.

for lack of ammunition, and the campaign would have taken longer to win – if, indeed, given the close-run thing that it was, it could have been won at all. Our ground crews worked in abysmal conditions and achieved a remarkable operating rate. By peacetime standards, by the end of the campaign, every helicopter in my Brigade Air Squadron was unserviceable – but they kept flying.'

All Marine flight training is done with the Army at their training establishment at Middle Wallop, Hampshire. Consequently no one has seen the need to design a distinctive Marine pilot brevet; instead, Marine pilots wear the wings of the Army Air Corps.

Perhaps it has something to do with the hybrid personality of the Royal Marines that their pilots are trained by the Army and their operating base is with the Royal Navy, at the Naval Air Station near Yeovilton, in the cider county of Somerset.

Brigade Air Squadron's headquarters are, if not exactly spartan, certainly utilitarian – an ivy-green collection of Portacabins but a short hover from their hanger and the control tower. In the hanger two of the squadron's Gazelles are to be found in various stages of dismemberment, while a crew is busily at work replacing the hefty main rotors of a Lynx.

'It's a rare thing to have all our aircraft serviceable,' remarks one of the NCO pilots. He continues, 'There are times when we have been pushed to get three Lynx airborne.'

Maintenance and ground-handling add to the operational complexities: while all the squadron's helicopters are maintained by Army engineers, such things as movement and refuelling are done by Marines. Bootnecks are a highly intelligent lot; why they cannot be trained as helicopter ground technicians no one is willing to say, for there appears to be little reason why the squadron should not be totally self-contained in the matter of aircraft maintenance.

It takes a great deal of money to train a Marine combat pilot: estimated flying costs of operating a Gazelle are £400 per hour and a Lynx, £1,600 per hour; so to train a Marine pilot to operational standards can cost the taxpayer as much as £100,000.

Much to the dismay of senior officers within the Corps, young pilots are increasingly being enticed out of the Marines into commercial flying. As one young officer says, 'There are some good deals in civilian flying. Some companies will even sponsor you through your civilian licences, so a lot of the guys are going on the outside; some are even shortening their time to get out. If I considered leaving

the Corps I would be looking at a £10,000-a-year pay rise.'

While pilot shortage is not at the moment a serious problem for the Marines, those in authority must recognize that if they cannot reverse the trend

of pilots departing for richer rewards – and, after all, who can blame them? – the Corps is going to be hard-pushed to meet its flying commitments should there be an international emergency in which it is required to participate.

With the tightening of military budgets, the Royal Marines are aware that their flying hours could be curtailed, so Marine pilots take every opportunity to maintain their operational effectiveness. Lynx helicopters fly low over the rich farmlands of Somerset during a navigation exercise.

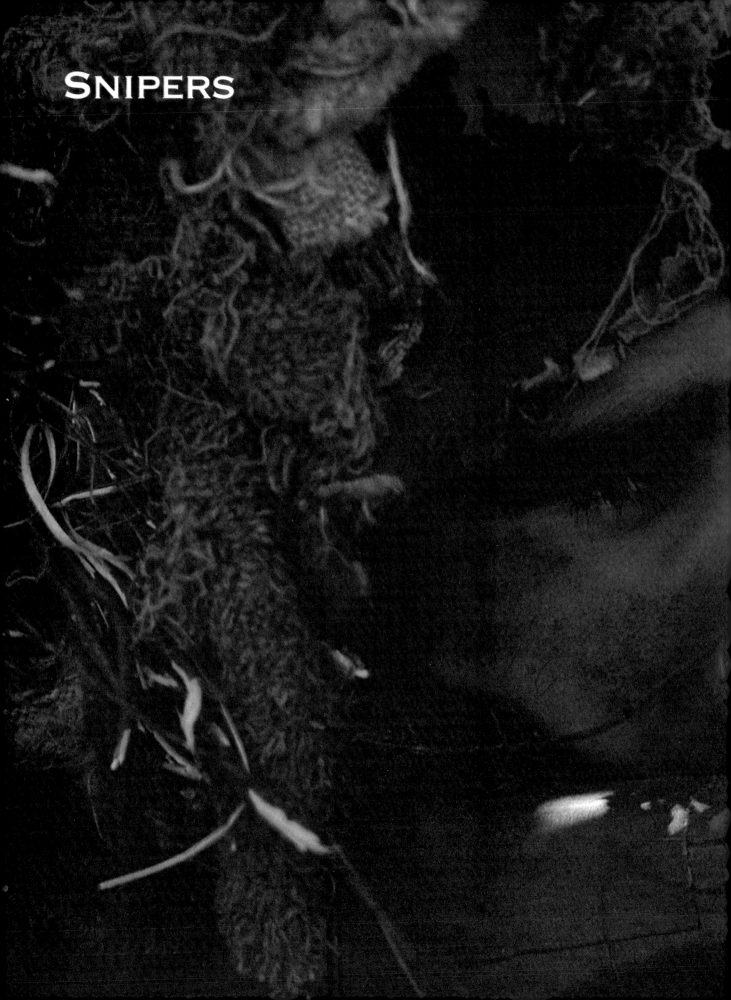

SNIPERS

To the layman there is something sinister and nefarious concerning the role of the sniper; the uninformed see it as a sorcerous art belonging to the world of hit-men and contract killing. In its military context, away from the make-believe world of Rambo, sniping is one of the oldest and most lethal forms of warfare. Others deprecate its use and, like fox hunting, see it as unsporting and unglorious.

It takes five weeks and four days to train a man to become a commando sniper, and the experts will tell you that the basic ingredients of a good sniper are patience and perseverance. Of the twelve students on the course probably only five or six will finally qualify. Why the low pass rate? One of the reasons is believed to be the lack of sufficient field skills by today's commandos.

'The Corps has changed during the last few years,' one of the instructors explains. 'We are now getting the four-year Marine. During this time he does not gain enough experience in basic fieldcraft skills to be sufficiently adept at becoming a good sniper. If you go back to the days when there used to be the nine-year Marine, he would have sufficient experience to attend a snipers' course and have a reasonable chance of passing it.'

There was a time when the sniper operated in solitary isolation, armed with a 303 Lee Enfield rifle equipped with a telescopic sight. Time has changed all that. Nowadays Marine snipers operate in 2-man teams: both men will be qualified snipers, but one will act as observer, the other as shooter. A sniper's weapon is personal and highly individualistic. While the United States Marine Corps sniper favours the M-40A1 sniper rifle, considered to be superior to the Remington M-40, which they used in Vietnam, Britain's Marine commandos prefer the 7.62mm L96A1, designed by Olympic champion Malcolm Cooper, which is fitted with a 6×42mm telescopic sight. It is a deadly weapon capable of providing a 10-inch group at 1,000 metres. Ammunition costs twenty-seven pence a round.

Commando snipers are trained to hit a target at 600 metres with a single shot. For his sniper badge test there are no 'zeroing' shots; he has to calculate wind strength and direction, estimate the correct elevation, then place a killing shot. Being an expert marksman certainly does not qualify a man to be a sniper. By the end of his training he is expected to hit targets at 1,000 metres. He must have the skill to stalk a quarry over long distances, navigate cross-country by day and night, and be a keen observer, capable of memorizing types of enemy armour, insignia and troop strengths.

Warrant Officer Tom Sands, a 20-year Marine, and a crack rifle shot with a warm country manner, feels that the Corps is losing its lead in the use of snipers, and that training in this form of warfare must be re-thought, if the Royal Marines are to remain serious contenders in the use of this skill. Nevertheless, as he says, 'The Royal Marine sniper is the most efficient and effective infantryman anywhere in the world, for the simple reason that he is trained to produce a one-shot kill up to a range of six-hundred metres, and he can crawl to within one hundred and fifty metres of a trained sniper observer and put down what would have been a killing shot, and still not be seen.'

Tom Sands is also a skilled tracker: he believes it is essential for a sniper to be able to read the ground and interpret the tell-tale signs that reveal when, and how many, people pass along a particular trail. He continues, 'There appears to be a serious lack of sniper awareness throughout the Corps, and I am sure that if Commanders understood how to employ them, and what their capabilities were, snipers would be a much sought-after and used supporting arm.'

A sniper's equipment has greatly improved with the advance of modern technology: rifles are now in use that can hit a target at 3,000 metres – nearly two miles – and there is ammunition that can penetrate 13mm of light armour. Nothing is safe from the well-concealed sniper these days: armoured vehicles can be rendered impotent by a well-placed sniper shot, through a driver's port or observation periscope, while anti-tank crews and mortar teams could suffer a similar fate. Even aircraft are vulnerable. Consider the damage a sniper could do from a 'hide' looking down on to an operation airstrip being used by troop-carrying helicopters.

Out on the wind-blown landscape of an autumn Dartmoor, Tom Sands watches his current batch of fledgeling snipers burrow away constructing hides; some are camouflaged in ghillie suits, which make them look like tattered scarecrows. They are still learning the fieldcraft tricks. He knows that only a handful will survive the course, but he is determined to instil in them all the skills that will make them into the world's finest commando snipers.

Previous page: No one would deny that the role of the sniper is a sinister and nefarious art. Experts claim that the Marine commando makes the world's finest sniper.

However, instructors admit that today's short-service Marine does not possess the same field-craft skills as were acquired by his predecessors.

PART 3

TO THE FAR ENDS
OF THE EARTH

FROM THE SOUTH CHINA SEA
TO THE SOUTH ATLANTIC

THE HONG KONG CONNECTION

Hong Kong is the most exhilarating place on earth. Should you savour its delights but once, your visit will be a tantalizing experience, for it is an island of bejewelled fantasies sparkling like a rare wine, amid a flurry of islands in the South China Sea. From the air on a clear day it is possible to see the length and breadth of this island of overwhelming contrasts; perhaps even further, beyond Kowloon to the bustling New Territories and distant Communist China, but a thin line on the distant horizon.

Nestling among the nooks and crannies of Victoria Peak are the sumptuous homes of the wealthy, while in the streets and alleyways below are the sleazy neon-lit bars of Wanchai and Causeway Bay. On this pinprick of land, rich and poor jostle side by side, each fighting to survive in their own particular world.

Cities, towns and villages, like people, have their own personality and spirit. Paris has a feminine charm and stylishness. Rome a feeling of the eternal. London, like the jaded star, clings to a Sixties' image long since gone. Hong Kong, on the other hand, reeks with a multi-layered vibrancy that makes the nerves quiver with youthful expectation. Such feelings were once reserved for New York's Manhattan Island, for the two cities have peripheral similarities. Both are islands with miles of shady, concertinaed waterfronts and mushrooming concrete and glass skyscrapers. Both have a climate that torments and, when seen from above, a weary population scurrying around in search of ever-increasing amounts of wealth. Both have their flamboyance and vulgarity. Over the years the poor and deprived of Europe have surged into New York to seek their fortune. Today, the poor and oppressed of Asia arrive on the shores of Hong Kong hoping to find freedom and the wherewithal to survive.

Throughout its history Hong Kong has always attracted a kaleidoscopic array of people. In its early days merchants became drug pedlars and used the colony's sheltered harbour as a useful stopover on their way to the Chinese ports of Canton and Shanghai. For a variety of reasons, an endless assortment of colonial civil servants was attracted by what was to become the glittering jewel in the Victorian crown. For the most part, it was an easy lifestyle for the small band of Whitehall bureaucrats, who no doubt relished the prospect of being pampered by an array of Chinese servants. There were others too: aspiring entrepreneurs, sea-going vagabonds, and soldiers of fortune of one kind or another. All were attracted to this small, rocky outcrop in the South China Sea.

Appalling as it may now seem, Hong Kong became British territory through the sale of opium. Shamelessly British merchants, supported by the Victorian Civil Service and the Navy, conspired to sell opium to the Chinese. Apart from silver, which was in short supply, the British, along with all the other European traders, had little else with which to barter, to obtain the luxuries they sorely needed from the Chinese. It was Chinese silk and tea after which the British hankered.

By 1841 the Chinese had been subdued by two opium wars and the superiority of an international force involving the British and Americans. As the dust of turmoil settled, the Victorians gained another piece of territory, along with 4,500 souls. That was well over a century ago. In the meantime Hong Kong, that once scraggy settlement in the South China Sea, had been transformed beyond its wildest dreams.

Behind the glitter and audacious wealth that everywhere flaunts itself, Hong Kong is plagued by an epidemic brought about by its own success – people. There are an awesome 5 million inhabitants in Hong Kong and the surrounding territories, and still the numbers grow. By the teeming boatload they come, searching for freedom and somewhere to lay their heads. At the rate of 500 to 600 a day, sometimes more, refugees and illegal immigrants are swarming into Hong Kong.

From war-ravaged Vietnam and its neighbouring countries, these weary humans scramble from their impoverished homes and ruined cities in search of a saner place to live. Opulent Hong Kong is the most obvious haven. Then, after surviving the torments and terrors of weeks at sea, their sanctuary turns out to be a Hong Kong detention camp. From inside their wire-fenced compounds silent, doe-like faces gaze out on to what must surely be, for them, a God-forsaken world.

Refugees are not a recent problem for Hong Kong. With the outbreak of the Tai Ping Rebellion in 1850, a stream of refugees from Canton fled to the new British enclave. Again in 1911, with the demise of the Manchu Empire, more refugees begged for a home on the island. So, for whatever reason, the oppressed of South-East Asia have seen the twinkling lights of a free capitalist Hong Kong and sought a better way of life there, and who can blame them. Surely it is no different from the Irish and European migration to the New World at the turn of the century?

Amid the glitter and flaunting wealth of Hong Kong remains the unsolved plight of thousands of refugees. A token Marine force still remains to assist the civil authorities.

Whatever time of day or night you arrive, the descent into Hong Kong's Kai Tak airport is wondrous. By night there are a myriad dazzling lights illuminating the city below; none of the enchantment is lost by day. From the aircraft, as if but an arm's length away, you catch the glint of spray against the hulls of junks making their way to some distant fishing ground. Then, when you are only a few hundred feet above the flimsy dwellings, the clamorous mass of Hong Kong unfolds below you. On the horizon, shimmering in the milky morning haze, it is possible to see the mountains and rice paddies of mainland China.

Towards the end of June it can be hot and humid, for it is just ahead of the typhoon season; for many, this time of year in Hong Kong can bring about a feeling of lethargy, regardless of the air-conditioned homes and hotels. Even old China hands despair.

Duties around the South China Sea are nothing new for Marines: together with the US Marines they defended Fort Halliday, strongpoint in the defence of the British Legation in Peking, at the beginning of the century. In 1857 a 2,000-strong force of Marines took part in the attack on Canton, and later occupied the Taku Forts at the entrance to the Pei-ho River. More recently, in Hong Kong, the Royal Marines have been assisting the civilian authorities – they work under the supervision of the Royal Hong Kong Police – in their campaign against illegal immigration. At the same time they keep a wary eye on all shipping traffic, as part of Hong Kong's fight against smuggling and narcotics operations, and over the years have made some spectacular finds.

The young Marine officer handles the car with great dexterity, weaving in and out of the mass of traffic. Like most cities in South-East Asia, there is hardly an hour of the day or night when there is not some form of life on the streets of Hong Kong. Ancient multi-coloured trams, with garish advertising along their sides, clang their way to the city centre. Handcarts, overladen with market produce, jostle amid taxis and buses.

'That's *Tamar* over on the right. From a distance it looks a bit like an upturned gin bottle. We've managed to get you a room there while you're with the squadron,' says the young officer. 'It's more convenient than the China Fleet Club down the road. You'll find the view from the mess something else.'

Apprehending illegal immigrants is not the Marines' only task. They are also on the look-out for narcotics and contraband.

HMS *Tamar* is the headquarters of the British military in Hong Kong. For some inexplicable reason it has always been a Navy custom to refer to all shore-based establishments as ships of Her Majesty's Fleet. Not only is this more than slightly incongruous, it can be downright misleading. When found, such 'ships' have, on occasions, turned out to be little more than a collection of down-at-heel Second World War Nissen huts. As anyone will tell you, HMS *Tamar* is not at all like

that for, without doubt, it is the finest hotel in Hong Kong. Being the inveterate colonialists that they are, the British have transformed *Tamar* into their very own national enclave, complete with its own small post office with ancient 'GR'-cyphered red pillar box, banking facilities from the Shanghai Bank (colloquially known as the Honkers and Shankers), chapel, gymnasium, the NAAFI that no self-respecting British garrison should be without, and a pocket handkerchief-sized lawn of matted,

coarse grass. Apart from the Chinese tailor, the hairdresser and trinket shop, everything is so prim and clannish.

Of course there is a luscious garden with well-manicured tropical plants and rose bushes, which is tended and watered regularly by a Chinese gardener. Near the harbour wall, under a large-leafed tree, is a small plaque to the memory of a former resident's pet dog. In the nearby swimming pool children screech with delight, while from the tennis

With the disbandment of the Marines' 3rd Raiding Squadron in Hong Kong, everyone realized, despite official denial, that the withdrawal from Britain's last colony had begun. Regardless of the political implications, it was a festive

event: a Marine band was flown in from Scotland, there was the usual immaculate parade, and the Commandant-General at the time, Lieutenant-General Sir Martin Garrod, took the salute and chatted with the officers and families.

courts comes the rhythmic plop of a ball followed by the occasional cultured cry of 'Good shot!' In the pale evening light, high up in the Prince of Wales's Building in the officers' mess, overlooking the moon-drenched panorama of Hong Kong harbour, officers in crisp white dinner jackets dine by candle-light with their ladies. It has all the atmosphere of the prevailing élite. A slice of England on the edge of China. And, of course, the British Embassy has let it be known that it would like the enclave to remain in British hands when the territory is reclaimed by Peking in 1997. As the Communists have refused to entertain the idea, idle teatime chat-ter has it that the British would rather blow up the building than surrender it to the People's Liber-ation Army.

Few people seem to be aware that the British military has already started withdrawing from Hong Kong. All that now remains is a token pre-sence to reassure all concerned that Britain will not relinquish her responsibilities before time.

Part of the withdrawal programme has involved the cutting back of the Royal Marines' presence in Hong Kong. Now only a handful of Marines remains from the once-potent, and highly success-ful, 3rd Raiding Squadron. At a time when Hong Kong needs all its resources to control the increas-ing numbers of illegal immigrants, the decision to disband a highly effective deterrent is regarded by many as imprudent and ill-timed.

During its eight years of operation the Royal Marines 3rd Raiding Squadron, comprising thirty-six Marines and twelve Chinese interpreters, car-ried out over 1,800 patrols, boarded over 4,000 various types of ship, arrested 954 illegal immi-grants and seized sixty-five boats.

Its origins go back to 1979, when the Govern-ment of Hong Kong realized that they were being swamped by illegal immigrants and that things were getting out of control. The normal yearly flow of 8,000 'illegals' had increased tenfold to an alarm-ing 80,000. It was not only a matter of the pathetic human cargoes arriving daily in frail, overcrowded craft, but of the devilish 'snakehead' syndicates, which, for vast sums – £2,000 or more – would smuggle women and children on to Hong Kong's shores, outwitting police blockades by their use of fast motor launches. Without outside specialist assistance, Hong Kong's marine police knew that the situation would become uncontrollable, so it was decided to call in the Royal Marines.

There are pitiful tales of women and children attempting to make a night dash across the South China Sea from some remote shore to what they hope is freedom in Hong Kong.

Imagine a moon-hidden night with a calm sea and a slight breeze. Somewhere on the Chinese mainland snakeheads stuff their human cargoes like layers of fish into the gutted bows of high-powered speedboats. No time is lost. Once loaded, the snakeheads speed towards Hong Kong's shores. They are spotted through the night-vision glasses of a Marine patrol. Marines have a gut feel-ing when snakeheads are going to make a run. Chal-lenging the boat, their quarry increases speed and tries to evade the Marines, who are about to over-take them in their specially designed Fast Patrol Craft (FPC). Both boats are now crashing through the sea at terrifying speeds – thirty, forty, fifty knots or more. As the Marines bear down on the smugglers, the snakeheads, realizing there is no escape, turn quickly and ram the Marine craft. Across the water echo the helpless screams of the human cargo. Four die. One Marine has both legs broken. Had it not been for the resourcefulness of the Marines, more would have perished. The snakeheads are jailed for twenty-five years.

Though much of the time spent patrolling the waterways and islands around the South China Sea was fraught with boredom, the Raiding Squadron had its successes and failures. One of these could have ended in tragedy, and was recalled by one of the Marines' senior NCOs.

As is often the case, it happened in the early hours of the morning, in the hazy uncertain light just before dawn. At the sight of a pursuing Marine patrol, a crew member of a junk, believing that they were about to be boarded by pirates, grabbed an AK 47 assault rifle and fired several bursts at the Marines. 'It shook us, I can tell you,' says the NCO, summoning a smile as he recalls the incident. 'For-tunately he fired above our heads, hoping to scare us off.'

The Marines, who were only lightly armed at the time, outmanoeuvred the junk, boarded the vessel, arrested the captain and frogmarched him to the armed crewman, who was instructed to surren-der his weapon. As it happened, this was no ordin-ary Chinese junk: it was manned by the Chinese militia and was carrying a wide range of weapons – everything from AK 47s and SKS rifles to a large-calibre Russian machine-gun, with a plentiful sup-ply of ammunition for all of them. As the NCO says, 'It all looked like becoming an international incident.'

Within the British enclave of HMS *Tamar* the Royal Marines of the 3rd Raiding Squadron bid farewell to the Hong Kong garrison.

He continues, 'It was all perfectly legal. The Chinese had licences for all the weapons, but they certainly weren't entitled to shoot at us in Hong Kong waters. After that we modified our tactics. Instead of approaching a boat in total darkness, which gave us the benefit of surprise, we had blue lights, a siren and a searchlight fitted to the boats. Before boarding any boat, we now switch on the blue lights and signal with the lamp.'

Naturally Marines are cagey when quizzed about the speed of the boats they use on these special operations.

'We had a few problems with them at first, overheating and that sort of thing,' says a former Warrant Officer. 'Now all that's been sorted out. Let's say they're pretty fast.' More than fifty knots fast? He smiles. 'Could well be,' he replies.

There is barely a ripple of breeze and the temperature is in the high eighties. Flags hang limply, contrasting with the soft, mist-laden sky that hangs around Hong Kong harbour.

It is 8.30 a.m. on 1 July 1988, and already the guests, in a variety of uniforms, are taking their places, some accompanied by wives and girlfriends. Everyone is dressed for the occasion. There are plain and floral dresses, some with scooped backs revealing gorgeous tans. Dainty hats, mostly brimmed and floppy, are everywhere. It is a time for white see-through gloves and wobbly, high-heeled shoes.

Within the hour the 3rd Raiding Squadron will be no more; disbanded like so many units of Britain's forces in recent years. At one end of the quay the Royal Marines Band, imported from Scotland for the occasion, is trumpeting a practice note and arranging its music, while the usual stream of military and civilian dignitaries takes its place. Toadying junior officials scurry to and fro like a flock of humming-birds. In their starched khaki tunics and white pith helmets, chin-straps and weapons glinting in the morning light, the 3rd Raiding Squadron is drawn up in precise rows. Not a foot or a chin-strap is out of place.

As a backdrop to this ritualistic military tableau are the sombre grey hulls of HMS *Swift* and *Swallow*, decorated, as is Navy tradition on these occasions, with a multitude of coloured flags and pennants. Like the Marines, they too are being dispatched to Britain, to be sold only eight years after they were brought into Hong Kong service.

When questioned on the Marines' and naval withdrawal, officials try to put a brave face on all this, refuting any premature departure and in-

ferring that, 'These routine adjustments to the strength of the garrison ... reflect the efforts of Headquarters British Forces to improve efficiency, cost effectiveness, and the sensible economic management of the garrison.'

It is all diplomat-speak – and everyone recognizes the fact.

At 9 a.m. precisely the parade begins. As parades go, it is a miniature affair. Royal Marines are used to bigger things than this. They are crowd-pullers, and they know it. Nevertheless, this small contingent of Marines performs with exact military precision, as if before the monarch in Whitehall with an audience of tens of thousands: ramrod backs, stark rasping commands, orchestrated feet wearing boots like mirrors – so bright you could shave in them. As the Commandant-General of Marines, Lieutenant-General Sir John Martin Carruthers Garrod, KCB, OBE, walks down the ranks, pausing to speak with each of his Marines, the band

Against the sumptuous background of Hong Kong, General Sir Martin Garrod, KCB, OBE, former Commandant General Royal Marines, takes the salute at the disbandment parade of the 3rd Raiding Squadron.

plays the old familiar melodies.

Much to the delight of everyone, after the customary march past, the Marines march around the compound to the strains of 'Colonel Bogey' and similar stirring tunes. Beyond the walls, Hong Kong is oblivious to the historic tableau being enacted within. As far as the Marines are concerned it is all so natural, for they have done it so many times before: they march past the deserted tennis courts and post office, past the aviary with its thirty or so chirping canaries and budgerigars and, with a flourishing ceremonial turn, crisply swagger back. They are proud, and oh!, so British. There are all the old familiar faces by now covered in small rivulets of sweat. As the crowds thin, an attractive young Wren officer remarks to her companion with a touch of sadness, 'It looks like the beginning of the end for all of us here.'

After the parade, like the company outing on its annual knees-up, group photographs are taken,

children are bounced on fathers' knees, and the General chats to wives and sweethearts. The squadron is having a family farewell party.

Operating from the Navy's two remaining ships in Hong Kong, a small contingent of Marines still remains to help in the fight against smuggling and illegal immigrants. Gone are the eight long hours of night patrols. New tactics have been developed: Marines are launched in their FPCs from the Navy's 'mother ship' when a likely target is suspected.

It is bewildering to try and understand the reasoning for the disbandment of the Marines' Raiding Squadron. They were a highly effective and successful extension of the civil power – the Royal Hong Kong Police – which will miss their expertise when their own manpower is overstretched in dealing with the illegal immigrant crisis.

Following the horrific events of Tiananmen Square, whoever resolved to disband the Royal Marines' Raiding Squadron must surely be reflecting on their folly. If the British Government was kowtowing to the demands of Peking, which was seeking a reduction of the Hong Kong garrison, it must now regret it. From the Communist position this would be seen as a weakening of Britain's bargaining power, making the Hong Kong Chinese even more vulnerable.

In the final analysis the premature reduction of the Hong Kong garrison could have serious consequences in the twilight years of Britain's last imperial outpost.

NORWAY
GUARDING THE NORTHERN FLANK

Each year as Christmas fades and a new year beckons, more than 4,000 men of 3 Commando Brigade pack up, lock, stock and barrel, and head for the frozen wastes of northern Norway in order to hone their fighting skills in a series of war games, in case, as one veteran Marine put it, 'The balloon goes up between us and old Ivan Ruskie.' Irrespective of a changing Europe, Britain's politicians, along with the military, still think in terms of confrontation.

Even in this missile-infested age, when one of these devastating weapons can cut a swathe through any advancing army, Britain's military 'brass', for reasons best-known to themselves, still believe that it is crucial to defend NATO's northern flank with conventional forces. *Glasnost* apart, the Marines believe that they have a vital role to play in the defence of this part of the world; even the United States Marine Corps (USMC), at all times reticent to concede that anyone can outfight them in any theatre of operations, is prepared to admit that the Royal Marines are the best in the world when it comes to Arctic warfare.

There could be a time, in the not too distant

Britain's Royal Marines are trained to overcome the harsh Arctic winters of northern Norway. As one instructor commented, 'First you learn to survive and live in this environment, then you are taught to fight in it.'

future, when the idea of defending the northern flank by conventional means will be considered too expensive and unnecessary. The Cold War politics of the past are being overtaken by more liberal doctrines – there is a wind of change, and the Warsaw Pact countries, as we have known them, will never be the same again. In the light of recent developments within the Eastern Bloc countries, the question must be asked: should NATO and the West not reconsider their defence priorities in this area now that the northern flank is no longer so vulnerable? There would always be a role for our special forces, such as the Marines: launched from submarines, they would operate as intelligence-gathering units and amphibious raiding forces, as they have done so successfully in the past.

For the time being, at least, the bitter winters of Norway with its beautiful, though bleak and hostile, landscape make an ideal Arctic training ground for our commandos. Youngsters unblooded in cold-weather training, and in the dangers of frostbite and hypothermia, are taught how to survive and fight effectively, travelling across the terrain on skis and snowshoes with 100-pound packs strapped to their backs. Weapons are tested, new tactics rehearsed, and vehicles driven through a hinterland normally considered to be impassable. It also provides the opportunity for our Marines to work with other specialist forces. On alternate years, following the brigade workout, a NATO exercise is carried out to test cohesion and effectiveness.

In the warm comfort of one of the winter chalets serving as company headquarters, a stocky mountain- and Arctic-trained NCO, a 15-year veteran of pitting his wits against the Norwegian winters, explains some of the training the first-timers have to undergo.

'We take a novice who does a basic three-week training course here in Norway and teach him how to ski; when he has acquired a good level of competence we put a pack on his back, and later expect him to navigate and ski at night. After three weeks he will be a proficient member of the company, capable of carrying out his duties as a fighting man in Arctic conditions.'

He pauses and continues.

'The individual must be able to survive before he can fight, he must learn how to dig snow holes, what wax to use on his skis, the kind of snow conditions he is going to meet, what distances he can cover. These are all of vital importance to his fighting abilities.'

Nothing is left to chance in training a young Marine for his first Arctic winter: in the beginning he will be exposed to perhaps only two or three nights in open terrain, where he and other members of the troop will build their own snow holes, learn how best to cook their Arctic rations and, most important of all, how to overcome dehydration. As he gains experience, so his nights in the Arctic environment will be extended, until he can be away on patrol for ten or more days, living off his specially prepared ration packs containing beef stock drinks, chicken supreme, oatmeal, nuts, raisins, chocolate drinks and a host of other mixtures, which are blended together and cooked on small naphtha-fuelled stoves – for paraffin will turn to jelly at low temperatures.

Norway can be regarded as the door to NATO's northern flank, and the Royal Marines have always regarded this Arctic terrain as their special area of operation. Now that confrontation with the Soviet Union has receded, and Cold War politics are regarded as obsolete, the Marines must re-evaluate their role in this area, in the light of the political changes in Eastern Europe.

It can never be said that the Marines are conventional or predictable when it comes to fighting tactics. Every Marine is taught to think for himself and is expected constantly to use his initiative. Most Marines, by their second winter in Norway, have become expert skiers. Others experiment with more unconventional military transport – the skidoo. While it can be a rapid form of transport over snow and snow-covered ice, traction can be lost when the skidoo hits icy slush. It is essential to protect the head, face and eyes (*left*) when driving one of these vehicles, for without face protection the driver can suffer frostbite within minutes. After an exercise on Lake Bessheim, a Marine NCO hurriedly debriefs his team while a SeaKing helicopter arrives with fresh supplies and the company mail (*right*). A senior member of the élite Mountain and Arctic Warfare Cadre demonstrates a firing position to Marines training to qualify for the M and A W speciality (*below*).

It is one of those winters when there is little snow; the streets of Oslo in January are similar to those of Paris or Madrid, with blue skies and warm sunlit days. The traditional Norwegian fairyland begins some 100 kilometres to the north, around Lillehammer. There is an omnipotence about this part of the world with its enchanting lakes and soaring, snow-capped mountains. The crunch of the snow as you walk through sweet-smelling pines is like nowhere else on earth; and were not Grieg and Sibelius inspired by the majesty of a landscape such as this?

It is a cold, steel-grey morning with a steady downpour of freezing rain and the temperature hovering at minus twenty degrees Centigrade. On the mountains nearby it has started to snow, and visibility is deteriorating. A SeaKing helicopter approaches out of the snowy mist; nearby on Lake Bessheim one of the senior NCOs of Sp Company is out evaluating a Lynx skidoo with a group of Marines. As the weather worsens they make their way through slush and ice to the lake shore.

Wrapped in Arctic clothing, the outer layers sodden from the melting icy rain, the patrol drags its machines up the bank, while the landing SeaKing causes the snow to swirl around them.

'These things are useless out there,' comments the leader, referring to the snowmobiles. 'With all this bloody slush around you can't get any traction on the ice.'

In one of the nearby lakeside chalets serving as a mess – they are rented to the Marines on an annual basis at a healthy profit by the local Norwegian community – there is the welcoming aroma of hot coffee and fried sausages and bacon. For visitors, and the newly arrived skidoo patrol, a welcome hot drink and a sandwich are always available for those with the right contacts in the kitchens. In a tight-knit commando unit there is always someone who knows somebody. It is a family that survives on the buddy system: find the right Marine NCO and he can get you anything from a sausage sandwich in an Arctic blizzard to a lift in a helicopter in the South Atlantic.

Let nobody be in any doubt that a Norwegian tour of duty is gruelling and dangerous. Beyond the camaraderie and the adventure of it all, the only reward is an extra living allowance: for example, 8.09 pence per day for a Corporal, 9.90p for a Captain. Regardless of age (and everyone will tell you that it's a young man's game), everyone – Marines, NCOs and officers – is exposed to the same gnawing hardships. Weather is the continuous all-embracing enemy in terrain where windchill factors can reach minus sixty degrees Centigrade, and a fall through the ice could result in death within minutes if the rules are not obeyed.

As the Gulf crisis intensifies, there is a growing

awareness within the British military establishment, concerning the lack of expertise in desert warfare. It is some twenty-five years since our Marines were engaged in Middle East operations. In preference to the annual 'yomp' to the Norwegian fjords, perhaps it is time to train for desert operations, in preference to waiting for the Soviet threat on the northern flank. By all means retain the Arctic expertise, but our Marines must adapt quickly to the sands of the desert. As they learnt their lessons on the Arctic from the Innuit peoples, so must they now search out the Bedouin and the Tuareg, and learn from them how to fight and survive in the desert.

After their initial training in learning how to survive and transport themselves in the Arctic terrain, Marines quickly learn how to improve their communal living. The 'buddy system' is essential for any degree of comfort. Rations are pooled, beef stew and chicken curry packs given added flavour with spices brought from home. For most Marines, their main meal will be in the evening. Cooking is done over a small chemical camp stove by a selected member of the group sharing the same bivvy or snow hole. While in the field, there is no need to endure a bothersome tooth. At company headquarters medical personnel cater for every emergency.

The British military cemetery at San Carlos Water is a beautiful, tranquil place, facing seaward and situated close to the settlement where Royal Marines of 40 Commando and members of the Parachute Regiment landed on 21 May 1982.

There are few men, if any, who are not, in one way or another, affected by war and conflict. Sometimes, though few hardened warriors would care to admit it, the change can be likened to a spiritual conversion similar to that of St Paul on the road to Damascus. Others may brood on the experience, re-living each moment, savouring every dramatic image of some gruesome battle. Even the battle-scarred veteran, once thrilled by conflict, will have second thoughts and will no longer cherish the idea of endless campaigning, for the reality of war means killing.

Whatever might be said about the various military strategies involved in regaining the Falklands – for there were some serious blunders as well as courageous victories – in retrospect there is no doubt that it was a commandos' war; with the exception of the Parachute Regiment, who have a similar kind of training to the Marines, it is generally acknowledged that many of the other troops who went south were ill-prepared for the bleak and savage conditions that awaited them when they landed in San Carlos Water in May 1982. Such observations by no means detract from the courage of any man or woman who went to the Falklands. Of fundamental significance is the fact that without the expertise of our commando forces, including the 2nd and 3rd Parachute Regiments, the Falklands campaign might well have resulted in a bitter fiasco, reminiscent of the ill-fated Dieppe Raid of the Second World War. From the military point of view, if ever there was a classic scenario for an amphibious commando operation in recent times, it was surely the Falklands landings.

It is nine years since the last fatal shot was fired: the acrimonious sounds of war have melted away; each side has buried its dead; and, as the feelings of bitterness and anguish diminish, the politicians emerge from their sanctuaries, like the hibernating creatures of the forest, to continue to debate the verbal conflict. Once more the islands are peaceful and docile, and the old familiar sounds have returned; gulls glide and swoop, their piercing cries echoing across San Carlos Water. The prevailing wind moves the long, coarse golden grass in rhythmic circles; by the shore, small waves create a gentle harmony as they rush against sand and pebble. Apart from the discordant note of a plopping engine, even the nearby settlement is silent; the sharp January sunlight illuminates the bright-coloured walls and roofs of weather-beaten homes with their peeling paint and Victorian-style lace curtains. Rising above the gentle rush of the wind and sea another sound is heard, resembling the

pealing of a muffled bell; it comes from the small military cemetery, remote and dignified in its wilderness setting, overlooking the bay. It is the sound of the ropes flapping against the flagpole supporting the red, white and blue Union Jack that crackles gently in the freshening breeze.

There are other reminders of the ravages of war. No longer can the islanders stroll carefree across the island's wind-blown landscape, for littering the countryside are thousands of unexploded mines and shells waiting to maim or kill the unwary passerby.

The Royal Marines are no strangers to the remote regions of the South Atlantic. A small detachment of about thirty or so – anonymously called Naval Party 8901 – were sent to the Falklands on rotating garrison duty when, in 1960, neighbouring Argentina began making serious demands that it be allowed to repossess the islands, which it claimed were its sovereign territory. The Marines made their base a few kilometres to the west of Port Stanley at the head of the waterway beneath the shadows of Mount Longdon and Tumbledown. They called it Moody Brook. Apart from the Royal Yacht *Britannia*, one of the most sought-after Marine postings, or 'drafts' as they call them, is to the Royal Navy's Ice Patrol Ship HMS *Endurance*, which carries out scientific research programmes while, at the same time, showing the flag in regions of the Antarctic.

Marines know that it is a once-in-a-lifetime opportunity to see and work in Antarctica, so there is keen rivalry to be part of this specialist detachment, which includes a Captain, three NCOs and nine Marines. The 6-month tour of duty is a long and arduous one; while on passage the Marines maintain watch along with other members of the crew. Once among the ice their Antarctic work is varied: they might assist surveyors ashore, provide stores parties, advise on safety equipment, accompany geologists operating from the ship, or provide search and rescue parties, should the need arise.

Fifteen members of the British Task Force, including seven Marines, are buried in the cemetery at San Carlos Water. Designed by the War Graves Commission and tended by the Property Services Agency, the cemetery was built mainly from local materials. Falklands stone and slate were used for the memorial wall, the perimeter wall and paving, while the headstones were made from limestone. Graves are bordered by clusters of seasonal flowers. The Royal Engineers, assisted by local labour, constructed the cemetery.

According to the Navy's handout:

> HMS *Endurance* has a ship's company of seventeen officers and 120 other ranks – including the Marines. The ship is named after a vessel in which the explorer, Sir Ernest Shackleton, sailed to the Antarctic in 1914; the following year it sank when it became trapped in ice in the Weddell Sea. The present ship was commissioned in 1968 and has been engaged in scientific work in Antarctica every year; she was involved in the Falklands campaign and was awarded, for her work in Antarctica, the 1982 Wilkinson Sword of Peace.

Down in the depths of *Endurance* several of the Marines are preparing to go ashore while the ship is revictualling for a few days in Port Stanley. One of them, an artist before he joined the Marines, is putting the finishing touches to a curvaceous pin-up, part of a large mural covering their clothes lockers. Another, a keen fisherman, is rummaging through his collection of flies for tomorrow's fishing trip, while others are attempting to read amid the boisterous banter of shipboard life.

One of the Marines, a stocky young Yorkshire lad – 'Ginge' to all his messmates – recalls how his commando training saved him from what could have been a hazardous situation.

'Me and the other lads had been out for a yomp, visiting one of the penguin colonies; on the way back I was map-reading, leading the lads across some snow, when all of a sudden I just disappeared down a crevasse. I finished up on a ledge. Below me were walls of sheer ice; above, a small hole through which I'd dropped. I was down there about twenty minutes and managed to get out with the help of a rope and me mates here.'

He relates the incident in matter-of-fact tones that make it sound as though it was all part of a day's work. No sweat – there was a problem and, between them, he and his friends managed to solve it. Without his mountain and Arctic training, it

Now that the ravages of war have disappeared, the Falkland Islands have returned to their timeless way of life. Sounds are muted: seabirds, the ocean, a flag flapping against the cemetery flagpole, with only the occasional discordant note of a farmyard engine. Advantages have been reaped from the islands' large military presence:

roads, communications and the economy have improved. The Royal Marines still have a presence on the islands; some have joined the local police, while others visit the Falklands by being selected to join HMS *Endurance* (*above*), the Antarctic survey vessel, which re-victuals in the Falklands during the ship's annual visit to Antarctica.

As in all British war cemeteries around the world, there is a peaceful dignity surrounding the memorial at San Carlos Water.

would almost certainly have been fatal.

Meanwhile three Marines, all in their early twenties, look out of the windows of a Sikorsky helicopter, and see for the first time San Carlos Water and the circular military cemetery lying close to the shore. They are making a pilgrimage to visit the graves of their comrades. None of them knew the men who died here, yet in another way they did, for the Marines lying here are 'family' – buddies they would like to have known.

As the sound of the helicopter fades beyond the distant hills they make their way through the knee-high grass to the cemetery gates. The sun is warm on their young tanned faces. A freshening wind blows up the channel from the South Atlantic, and above the sky is blue, near cloudless. As they open the wrought-iron gate it creaks; they close it gently and look around. They stand, each with his own silent thoughts; the wind ripples the wreaths of red poppies at the foot of the memorial. Every so often the silence is broken by the flapping of the crisp new flag above them. They wander among the graves, stooping here and there to draw aside a clump of lupins or marigolds to read a name. They take their photographs and chat quietly, looking seaward, the way their comrades had come.

Silently closing the cemetery gate, they wander to the water's edge and amble off into the distance behind a small headland. Overhead a solitary gull circles in the updraft, its wings edged with the light of the afternoon sun, and the golden grass ripples in the wind.

PART 4
THE WORLD IS OUR STAGE

BEATING RETREAT
WHITEHALL, LONDON

His Royal Highness The Prince Philip, Captain General Royal Marines, watches the Beating Retreat ceremony.

It is a balmy summer's evening in June. Through the lacy greenery of St James's Park shafts of creamy sunlight filter through the branches, creating soft, moving patterns on the pavements. June is a busy month in London. Already the holiday ferment is in full swing. Along the Mall the crowds have thinned and now meander to brightly lit Piccadilly and Regent Street. In the park deck-chairs are scattered in woeful disarray. Here and there, oblivious of everything around them, lovers embrace and caress. For the most part life along the borders of Horse Guards Parade is reverent and genteel. Not here will you catch the whiff of burnt sausage and onions, for vendors will be given short shrift by vigilant parks police. Horse Guards and St James's are hallowed ground. Some would have you believe this is a male preserve, as were, until recent times, the clubs but a stone's throw away; the Travellers', the Reform and the Athenaeum.

There is an exaggerated quality of life around Horse Guards. Men with military gait, some well suited, others slightly bedraggled and poorly pressed, purposefully striding out with tightly furled umbrellas, make their way to the Admiralty, Whitehall and the neon-lit corridors of the Foreign Office. It is hardly surprising to see a sprinkling of regimental and old school ties and a jauntily placed bowler, though these days this mufti conformity is giving way to tired trilbies, Scots tweed and cavalry twill. The once obligatory white handkerchief discreetly placed in top pocket will now be a Liberty or paisley silk. Parchment-stiff white collars have been replaced by neat button-down shirts from Gieves & Hawkes. This is the civilian uniform of those who inhabit the rabbit-warren of offices that surround this heartland of Government and the nearby military garrison.

For three evenings in June, with the assistance of the men from the Department of Public Works, Horse Guards will be transformed into a giant amphitheatre. Thousands will be treated to an orgy of military pomp and musical excellence. Overnight, seats to accommodate them have been created from miles of interlocking scaffolding and wooden benching. Here and there flags ripple in the warm summer air. An hour or more before the performance the crowds gather, some winding their way from the Mall, others through the small arch leading on to the square from Whitehall, where it is said that King George II rode, after it was refurbished by William Kent during the middle of the eighteenth century. Amid all the military razzmatazz, there is a great deal of saluting and handshaking. Vivacious women in flimsy, swirling dresses wearing a mixture of hats, brimmed and cloched, gloved hands clutching expensive Italian bags, walk sedately across Horse Guards accompanied by husbands, sons and lovers. Throughout the day security has been tightened. It may be an occasion for some, but others are scornful of these military goings-on. An irritated bus conductor mutters to a passenger, 'As if we didn't have enough problems at this time of night without this lot.'

For the homeward-bound their favourite meander across Horse Guards and through the park to Victoria is threatened. Only ticket-holders, VIPs and a small clutch of cameramen are being given access from Whitehall. Meanwhile, a stone's throw away at Wellington Barracks, some 400 Marine musicians make last-minute preparations for the evening's performance. Snow-white helmets and tunics are carefully adjusted, instruments trilled and music shuffled into order.

Regardless of whether you have a particular military bent, Beating Retreat is an especially moving spectacle. Watching it, many undergo a deep personal experience approaching the religious.

The Sovereign's husband, Prince Philip, is Captain General of the Royal Marines, and this year Beating Retreat is being performed to celebrate his birthday. Like so many military traditions, Beating Retreat originates from early warfare, when a drum – used for battlefield signals – beat the signal to retreat to warn outlying troops to withdraw to their encampment before the pickets were set for the night. As far as we know, the custom is first recorded in the sixteenth-century document *Rules and Ordynaunces of the Warre*, where it is referred to as 'Watch Setting'. Again we find the ceremony mentioned in Humphrey Bland's eighteenth-century work *Treatise of Military Disciplin*, where it states that:

> Half an hour before the gates are to be shut, generally at the setting of the sun, the drummers of the Port Guard are to go upon the ramparts and beat a retreat to give notice to those without that the gates are to be shut.

Recognized as the world's finest ceremonial fanfare trumpeters, these Marines thrill audiences at hundreds of public performances in Britain and overseas each year.

94

From its battlefield usage a musical setting has emerged that was first performed on Gibraltar in 1934.

There is no escaping the fact that Beating Retreat is pure theatre and, like the artists at Covent Garden or the Bolshoi, Marine musicians are dedicated performers. Lovers of military band music will tell you there is nothing to compare with a Marine band. Likely as not the Guards, and other similar bands, will ridicule this claim.

On Horse Guards the ceremony is about to begin. Late-comers are shuffling along the aisles, desperately searching for their allotted seats. Old hands who know the discomfort of Ministry of Works seating bring cushions and plaid blankets to ease cramped limbs. Here and there the occasional falsetto voice rises above the murmuring of the crowd: 'My dear, how lovely to see you again . . . it's been simply ages. . .was it Sybil's wedding?'

Such classic county accents seem dated and out of place. Current phone numbers are exchanged and hurriedly stuffed into Gucci bags. Across the park, from the direction of Wellington Barracks, the bands have begun to play. Harsh commands echo through the trees, causing a flight of pigeons to take to the air in a rhythmic, circling formation, alighting on a higher vantage point on one of the Admiralty buildings nearby.

As the Horse Guards clock chimes the half-hour, the white-helmeted bandsmen swing on to

the parade ground playing 'Sarie Marais', an old South African melody associated with the Boer War. With gymnastic precision and swank, the pageant moves harmoniously through a series of complex marching formations. On all sides, banked rows of spectators appear apparently mesmerized by the beauty of the music echoing and re-echoing among the trees and buildings, as the last rays of mellow light slip behind the terraced grandeur of the Mall. All the conventional tunes are played: 'HM Jollies', 'The Captain General' and 'Preobrajensky', a slow march named after the Russian Foot Guards with whom the Mountbatten family is believed to have had ties. Like all good theatre, the whole performance reaches a climax in the final act. Now the pace changes. Where there was pomp and ceremony, interspersed with harmonious melody, a more sombre note prevails. Once more the atmosphere is transformed; Horse Guards has an ethereal quality about it. In near silence, the assembly senses a communal spirituality. Nothing moves. Neither the pigeons, the flags, nor the people. In hallowed unison the massed bands play 'Abide With Me'. Out into the stillness of the evening the familiar refrain carries into the city beyond. One last flourish remains: the Marines' ceremonial trumpeters play the haunting lament 'To Comrades Sleeping'. Many in the stands bow their heads in silent tribute. Even foreign visitors and those opposed to national pomp look on in silent awe.

THE SCHOOL OF MUSIC

While the Marines mourned the death of their comrades, the daily programme at the Royal Marines' School of Music continued.

We live in the age of the terrorist – fanatical men and women who believe they have a justifiable cause for which they are prepared to die. Terrorists have no regard for who they kill or assassinate in order to gain publicity for their evil campaigns. Families have been murdered; children, the elderly and even animals have been the targets of terrorist savagery. The nature of the terrorist is to strike at the weak, the unprotected and the unsuspecting. Defenceless targets are their stock-in-trade, which they eliminate with bullet or bomb. One such target was the Royal Marines School of Music, at Deal in Kent.

On the morning of Friday 22 September 1989 a horrendous explosion demolished a school building used by Marine musicians during their practice periods. Eleven Royal Marine musicians died. The IRA claimed it was the work of one of their active service units in Britain.

Amid the dust and rubble, Marine musicians, along with their officers and NCOs, clawed their way through the remains of the shattered building in an effort to rescue their comrades. The small seaside resort of Deal went into mourning. Each home

felt it to be a personal tragedy. Within hours floral tributes were arriving at the main gates. Children came with their parents, clutching small bunches of flowers, and placed them alongside the barrack walls.

It was a bitter loss for the Royal Marines. A week later, to the delight of everyone, and in defiant mood, the band proudly marched and played its way through the town of Deal. In memory of their murdered comrades, open spaces were left in their ranks to mark the place where they should have been playing.

In coloured crayon, a note written by a child was attached to the barrack walls, surrounded by flowers. Its message read: 'Please God, we do not forgive the IRA, they do horrible things to our band. Why do they bomb? We do care. We do care – Amen.'

At the Royal Marines' School of Music in Deal, a handsome, if somewhat dilapidated collection of nineteenth-century buildings, an old soldier recalls how it used to be in his day as a musician. Terry Williams is fifty-four, grey-haired and moustached.

Each morning Marine musicians rehearse a varied selection of music, from a Sousa march, to Ravel's Bolero.

He has a lined, weather-beaten face that reveals humour and generosity, he is articulate and a good story-teller. In one way or another he has been part of the Marine 'family' for the past forty years. He started as a boy musician and finished as a Warrant Officer Band Master. Unable to sever the 'umbilical', as he calls it, he is now an expert woodwind repairer.

'When I joined, I received half a crown a day – one pound, seven and sixpence a week. You used to draw seven and sixpence and the rest was compulsorily saved. I couldn't afford to send anything home out of that. In those days we wore blue serge for ordinary working dress, with a button-up tunic and collar. Imagine what it was like on a hot day. Our trousers were very scratchy, so were the flannelette shirts. In my time, there were 400 boys and staff in these barracks, today there are perhaps 100 people on an occasional basis. These days the emphasis on training has changed. They do more military training than we used to. For us it was all music and education.'

British brass bands, in particular military ones, are the envy of everyone the world over. Some might claim that it has something to do with our colonial past and our inbred xenophobic nature. It is hardly surprising that the Marines inherited their musical tradition from the Royal Navy, and in one way or another music-making has been an essential ingredient of all naval social and warring occasions. Sir Francis Drake, no doubt to assist in overcoming the social deprivations he endured while colonizing for Britain, enlisted a player of the viol – a forerunner of the violin – to accompany his ships' trumpeters. Previously Drake had sailed to Spain and Portugal with a band from Norwich made up of a sackbut, three hautbois and a treble recorder.

At the time of Trafalgar (1805) it appears that the captains of the fleet began to appreciate the need for music in their ships' companies. Britain's enemies, notably the Dutch, French and Spanish, being less stoical, had already felt a need to have their sea-going days enlivened by music of some kind. As the British fleet bore down on the French and Spanish men-of-war, musicians on Nelson's *Victory*, it is reported, played the National Anthem,

Every note, drum beat and step must be precise. Marine musicians are instilled with the ethic of perfection.

'Rule Britannia' and 'Britons Strike Home'. When musicians of the day were taken prisoner they were treated as little more than the plunders of war. When Rear-Admiral Mitchell had surprised the Dutch fleet in 1799, his social life was enhanced by the addition of sixteen Dutch musicians who, before regaining their freedom, entertained the Navy for the next two and a half years.

It is strange that the Royal Marines' School of Music is always referred to as being at Deal, for to be geographically accurate it is much nearer to Walmer. From the barrack walls you can see the Walmer lifeboat perched proudly on the pebbled beach nearby. Be that as it may, this sleepy part of Kent has been the centre for the training of Marine musicians for nearly fifty years. This nearly forgotten part of the Kent coast, with its ageing guest houses, dilapidated pubs and garish trinket shops, is a retirement area, and little visited apart from the annual holidaymakers who faithfully return each year. Bypassed by the endless streams of trucks, cars and caravans threading their way to the pleasure spots of France and Spain, Deal and Wal-

mer lie to the north of the M20 between Dover and Ramsgate. Just how much longer the Marine musicians will remain here is difficult to ascertain. Town and barrack gossip says that the School of Music is to be moved. Meanwhile the Mayor and city fathers are fighting to keep the Royal Marines' School of Music in their town, which, with customary Kentish pride, they have come to regard as their very own.

These days, a timeless charm surrounds the old barracks. Weather-beaten blackened bricks support lines of uniform, period windows. There is an austerity about the place that reflects confinement and incarceration. Nowadays the young musicians live in modern dormitories, six to a room, a drum roll away from where generations of youngsters have learnt their music. On walking through the old barracks, every creaking stairway and corridor appears to echo with the sound of cornet, drum and clarinet. Listen with care and you could hear the ghostly sounds of Mozart, Haydn and Sousa percolating through the passageways of this ancient place. Victorian austerity and sparseness prevailed

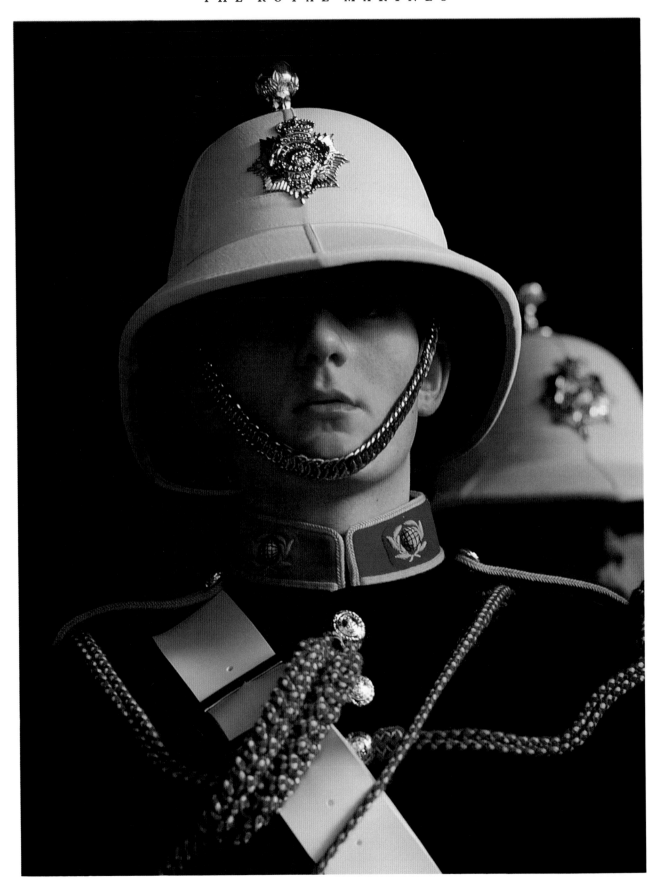

well into the 1950s, and there remains a macabre quality about these buildings, where the sallow spring sunlight casts strange shadows into every corner. These were hardly halcyon days for recruit musicians in their hirsute uniforms, and with a meagre few shillings for pay. Instruments were kept under beds, the barracks were their practice rooms, and coal fires at each end of the Dickensian accommodation provided the only heating. Large, shimmering black supplies of coal were kept in the nineteenth-century bins, thankfully today used as flower tubs.

Every year a group of anxious teenage youngsters, pink-faced and eager, their 'civvy' hairstyles shaggy and uncropped, passes through the gates of the Royal Marines' School of Music, Deal, with the high hopes of becoming military musicians. In confidence, most will admit to being inspired by watching and listening to one of the Marine bands on some public occasion. It may have been at Earls Court, Eastbourne's bandstand, or perhaps the hallowed moments by the Cenotaph each November as the Marine trumpeters play in memory of the fallen. No matter the place, each will have imagined himself, white-helmeted and blue-suited, being part of the Marines' panoply of music.

No promises are made by the Marines to its aspirant musicians when it comes to instrumental choice. Naturally, if a young man has spent several years playing the bassoon or violin, the Corps will make every effort to build on his expertise. After all, training costs money, and when military budgets are being scrutinized, musicians will tell you that bands are where the hatchet falls first.

By joining the Marines these young men will, after thirty months of intensive training, become professional musicians devoting the next twenty or so years to music and ceremony. The achievements of the Marines during their training period are quite remarkable, considering that most music students spend almost twice that time at any conservatory of music, refining years of childhood practice. As a trained musician, a Marine will be able to switch from brass compositions to concertos and jazz with fluent dexterity.

In the days prior to the demise of the Empire most of Her Majesty's ships had their own bands. All that is past. Now, instead of joining a ship, a newly qualified musician will become a member of one of the Corps' seven bands.

Affectionately called a 'Bandy' by the rest of the Corps, the junior musician is well aware that he will never wear the coveted green beret, or the parachutists' brevet worn by his fellow-Marines elsewhere.

As far as he is concerned, he is neither commando nor infantry soldier. Their officers, on the other hand, will most certainly disagree. As far as they are concerned, 'Bandies' – regardless of their non-green-beret status – are fighting musicians and very much part of the commando force. Much to the chagrin of many senior musicians, promotion is determined not only by musical skills but by knowledge of infantry tactics and beach landings – a far cry, they feel, from their chosen vocation of music.

A veteran bandmaster, now retired from the Corps, gave me an insight into the feelings of the musicians. 'It's the politicians who have tried to turn the band service into something that it isn't – fighting musicians. To appease them and the Treasury, bandsmen have been given a military role for which they are not suited. Do you realize that a Band Sergeant is required to know all the details of landing a commando on a beach? There's no way, no matter how bad things get, that a Band Sergeant is going to be called upon to act as a beach master for landing a commando.'

To dispel any thoughts the young student might have regarding his status, the military ethic is instilled into him from the moment he arrives at Deal. As one instructor said, 'We don't want them getting any fancy ideas that this is an exclusive conservatory of music – all gigs and no discipline!'

Many will be disappointed that their instruments are not awaiting them. That will come later. For the first eight weeks they will not touch an instrument. It will be all drill and physical fitness. In its glossy band service brochure the young 'Bandy' is reminded that, 'Although the band service is a musical body, it is first and foremost part of a larger military organization – The Royal Marines.'

Talk to any of the instruction staff at Deal and they will tell you that they have a serious problem. There is a critical shortage of Marine musicians. Regardless of their glamorous high profile, their ability to create some of the world's finest band music, young men are not being attracted to military music as a career.

In a tavern near the barracks a senior musician says, 'We can't recruit, we are about fifty under strength – on the musical side I can see us being cut again.' He goes on to explain further. 'Young lads these days are taught to look at a package. There is no overtime in this service. As a bandsman you can get in the coach at six in the morning and not get back to the barracks until two the following morning. No civilian works the hours we do.'

When asked why there are no black musicians

'It's meant to look easy, but it takes hours of constant practice,' was the comment of one drum instructor. Marine Drum Majors who, on ceremonial occasions, lead the parade, are selected from the Corps Drums and Bugle section.

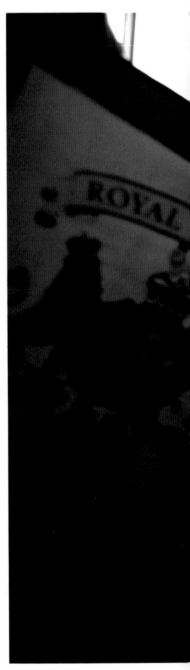

in the band, since they are so talented, he takes a long swig of beer, smiles faintly and says, 'Well, it wouldn't look right, would it, black faces under a white helmet – the "brass" wouldn't go for it.'

Marine bandsmen, like their commando counterparts, are selected with great care and deliberation. Any aspiring musician should be aware that being able to squeeze a few harmonious chords from grandfather's old melodion will barely suffice. String players and pianists, on the other hand, have a distinct advantage, as the Marines are well aware that to achieve any degree of professional pro-

ficiency in these instruments can take far longer than the available training time allows.

Like any conservatory of music, aspiring musicians are auditioned before being accepted for training. For three days Marine and civilian instructors delve into the boys' background to ascertain their suitability.

'We are not looking for musical geniuses,' said one of the staff, 'but a lad with appreciation of rhythm and harmony. There must be something musically aware in the young man – something we can build on.'

Between them, the instructional staff have accumulated hundreds of years of expertise. They know what they are looking for. A number of the civilian instructors will have played with the world's greatest orchestras and taught at internationally known colleges of music. Many of the Marine instructors will have travelled the world playing at festivals and great sporting events, as well as entertaining the Queen and her guests aboard the Royal Yacht *Britannia*. At each audition the Marines will scrutinize the young man's musical knowledge. He will be aurally tested and asked to

Trainee musicians are expected to spend many hours in private practice. On any day of the week the visitor may hear a familiar piece from a concerto or popular refrain, being played on the oboe, violin or trumpet, resounding down the ancient corridors of the Royal Marines' School of Music. Practice space is

scarce, so a secluded corner by a window is a prized location. A cellist foregoes a lunch break to perfect a solo he is playing at an evening concert. While barrack-room playing is frowned upon, two students take the opportunity to practise in their deserted dormitory.

write down the rhythm of a simple tune, identify major and minor chords and name the interval between notes.

Any young man who dreams one day of being a Drum Major and leading a Royal Marine band will, more than likely, have been selected from the bugle and drums section. It takes twenty months to train a bugler, a year less than a musician. During this time he will be taught to play the bugle, side-drum and the flamboyant E-flat herald trumpet. Many will have played with cadet and marching bands before joining the Marines. No Royal Marine band would be complete without its buglers and drummers. On ceremonial parades, public events and Royal occasions these are the men that the public see first; line abreast, with gleaming side-drum and bugle, marching with a self-confident swagger behind the Drum Major. Although they are an integral part of the band service, the drums and bugle section has a different rank structure and a variance in uniform. Buglers wear a thin red stripe down the side of their uniform, in contrast to the broad stripe worn by musicians.

'By term two – after fifteen weeks of training – if they have survived, they are ours for life.'

This is the general opinion of most of the teaching staff at Deal. Even then, however, some students could still be 'binned', as the Marines call it, for not possessing the musical flair and determination that the Corps demands.

It is a lovely English autumn morning; crisp air that condenses as you speak. Mellow sunlight and leaves fall and drift at the approach of winter. The Drum Major is the archetypal drill instructor with the familiar patter of a bygone age. He scans the lines of young musicians playing the popular melody 'We Are Sailing' as they march up and down the parade square.

'Watch your dressing...give me straight lines...I want lovely straight lines!'

He leans forward slightly, pace-stick tucked neatly under his left armpit as he bellows again.

'You're not giving me the lines I want – straighten them. About turn, 'ALT ... we're bloody awful this morning, aren't we?'

There's not a move from the rosy-faced youngsters.

'Right! We're all out 'ere until we get it right...Quick march...'eef 'ight, 'eef 'ight, about turn, 'eef 'ight...'

His voice peals out above the sound of the lilting refrain. This age-old parade-ground ritual continues, as it has done since time immemorial for

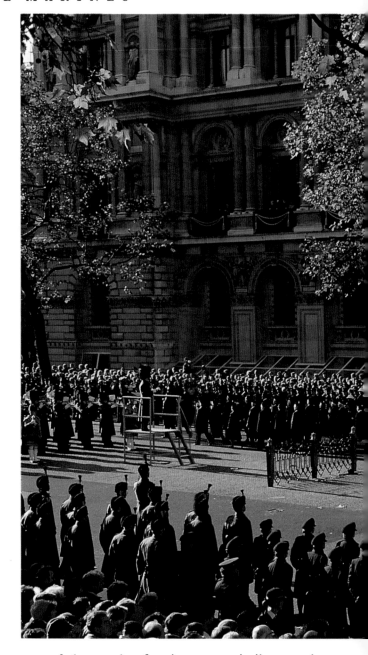

tens of thousands of trainees, on similar parade squares from Aldershot to Chittagong. The patter of Drill Sergeants never changes. Still the same dry wit, darting eyes and twitching moustache. Only the face seems to alter.

Simultaneously the Band Master moves silently between the ranks of marching musicians. He is the Master; the boys call him 'Sir'. Hands behind his back, lightly holding a conductor's baton, he listens intently for any discordant notes. It is said he can detect a slithered phrase or misplaced minim at a hundred paces.

As the morning routine changes into a series of complex counter-marching, the rows of sensitive

faces, barely visible beneath glossy peaked hats, take on a keener, more intense look. Instinctively they are aware that the eyes and ears of the two instructors are watching every move – never missing a note. An increased sense of awareness and purpose pervades. By the musicians' easy swagger and lightness of tone, almost a trademark of Marine bands everywhere, one is mindful that the pageantry process is taking shape. To the casual observer it all looks so simple.

'It must look easy to look good,' the Band Master remarks after the parade. 'We're continually seeking ways to improve our standards and our public performance.'

At the annual Service of Remembrance, held at the Cenotaph in London's Whitehall, Royal Marine buglers participate by sounding the Last Post and Reveille. Witnessed by thousands, and heard by a worldwide audience, the Remembrance Day parade is only one of over 1,500 public performances in which Marine musicians take part throughout the year. There are seven Marine bands which, each year, give a variety of concerts to an international audience: while one may be playing at a royal garden party, another could be on tour in Australia, and a third playing to holiday visitors gathered around the Eastbourne bandstand.

At any one time there might be eighty to ninety young trainee musicians at Deal. The school not only trains its future bandsmen, but is also the centre for a continuous round of training for Band Corporals, Sergeants and Band Masters. Overseas students are frequently sent to the Royal Marines for training as musicians and conductors. At one concert in the barracks church of St Michael and All Angels, the conductors for the evening included a Warrant Officer from the Bahrain Defence Force and another from the Oman Royal Guard.

The students' week is divided into forty-four periods, and they will have a 12-hour day, beginning at six in the morning. Most will be learning two instruments; the Marines call it being 'double-handed'. Inevitably a number will fall by the way-side – for some it is the continuous pressure of musical training within a military environment; for others it is simply homesickness. But the time-tested precepts of Marine musical training remain. There will be one-to-one tuition by civilian professors, as often as twice and sometimes three times a week, lasting forty minutes or more. The student will hear the word practice, practice, practice and more practice until he wearies of it. Like the Olympic athlete, he will undergo a daily improving and refining of his skills. Instructors who play the same instrument will closely monitor his progress; helping, cajoling, encouraging. It could be said, perhaps, that the students are not indulged with large helpings of musical theory. But then, where else in the world can you be taught to play two instruments to concert standard in thirty-two months?

Rightly, it is believed that this is an unimaginably difficult learning programme for student musicians. Consider also the versatility of these young men: not only are they bandsmen but orchestral performers as well. Their musical dexterity has to be heard to be believed. In one concert performance they played Sousa's 'Semper Fidelis', excerpts from Rossini's *The Barber of Seville* and a swinging Latin American dance number. Some have formed their own groups. At Christmas they play carols for charity, at other times they will organize a jazz or rock gig in a local tavern or dance hall.

The task of keeping the bands constantly supplied with new music falls on the staff of the music library. With only a handful of employees and two computers to assist in transposing, writing, arranging and composing, the library endeavours to meet the needs of all the Corps' seven bands. Like most of the Arts in Britain, from opera to the theatre, Marine bands are subjected to tight budgeting. To

Trainee musicians are frequently reminded that they are first and foremost Marines – then musicians. To underline this point recruits accepted for training as musicians are first given military training. It is equally important for a musician to be fit as it is for a Marine. Sometime during the year all Marine musicians take part in a military exercise to maintain their infantry skills. While young musicians are taught precision on the drill square, precision of a different kind takes place in the instrument repair workshops. Here, a small group of highly experienced specialists, some former musicians and bandmasters, restores, repairs, and services the Corps' extensive inventory of instruments with infinite care.

meet all their needs and to supply arrangements for seven bands, the music department of the Royal Marines has a meagre annual budget of £10,000. Expenditure has to be planned with infinite care, when a popular set of music such as that for *Les Misérables* can cost £55. The Marines' music library contains 14,500 musical scores; a considerable amount of music. Of course it is never enough, when you consider the number of performances that the Marines play around the world each year.

As you would expect with any military organization, the inventory of back-up equipment is an important factor. According to rough estimates there are 2 million pounds' worth of instruments available to bandsmen – including those on issue to them. However budget-conscious the Marines are, instruments are expensive and prices rising. Take a double E-flat bombardon, for example: to replace this could cost in excess of £2,500. Stores personnel say that they have several instruments valued at £15,000 or more. Certain instruments are available which give that clearer clarity of note, a richer quality, than the run-of-the-mill stores issue. These are given to selected players, perhaps a soloist or a devoted player who can make the instrument 'sing' in his hands. In an emergency, the Marines' music store is capable of re-equipping a complete band or orchestra within hours.

Nearby, a small team of specialist craftsmen repairs and refurbishes unusable instruments. One is a former bandsman, another played strings with an international orchestra until he became tired of wearing a dinner jacket for most of his life. Nothing is too complex for this dedicated team: with miniature tools specially adapted to their needs, watchmakers' lathe and welding torch, they weave their spell of experience on battered trombone and ageing fiddle. One cleans the valves of a Boosey & Hawkes trumpet while his companion, like a surgeon involved in a delicate operation, totally dismantles, piece by piece, a Schreiber bassoon.

Once a young musician's training is complete, the pace and intensity of his daily life will not change – merely vary. Frequently there will be two, and sometimes more, concerts in a day, with little time for detailed rehearsal. For the next twenty years – a bandsman is expected to retire at forty – his life will be devoted to a kaleidoscope of music-making. His music will be in demand to the far ends of the earth. He will perform before monarchs and presidents, princes, sultans, peers of the realm and, most of all, to Tom, Dick and Mabel on the village greens and bandstands throughout the kingdom. All the world's his stage: his platform will range

from the flight deck of aircraft carriers and palaces, to garishly lit shopping malls and London's Albert Hall. As a Marine musician he will become one of the most sought-after entertainers on the global circuit. He will also be among the world's most underpaid performers. . .

Change will undoubtedly come to the Royal Marine band service during the course of the next few years.

'As musicians become increasingly difficult to recruit, it is only a question of time before the first women are enlisted in the band service,' said a former Director of Music convincingly.

While none of the Marine hierarchy will admit to any future cutbacks in the number of bands,

there is an inevitability about reductions. Within the ranks of musicians, most will confess to the wind of change blowing in their direction. With watchful eyes on military spending, some White-hall 'pennypinchers' may feel that maintaining a sprightly, youthful Marine band service is a luxury the nation can ill afford. There would be many who would say that such thinking was heresy. Marines and their music are renowned the world over: they are, after all, a quintessentially British institution. Royal Marine music should be allowed to grow and flourish. Their performances enhance the quality of our lives and transplant the flavour of our national heritage to the far corners of the earth. Wherever they go everyone is musically richer for it.

Amid the sumptuous surroundings of a Hong Kong shopping area, in the Central District, lunchtime crowds are entertained by the music of a visiting Royal Marines band. Dressed in their white tropical dress, never seen in Great Britain, the Marine musicians delight a crowd of several hundred by playing a selection of popular music, including jazz, some Caribbean numbers and well-known Gershwin melodies. As a finale the Corps of Drums gives a vivid display that mesmerizes everyone. One expatriate was overheard saying, 'That certainly beats the Guards band that was here recently.' When on tour, Marine musicians will frequently play informal 'gigs' for their own mess or in a local tavern.

THE
CHRISTMAS
PANTOMIME

Can you imagine it? Hulking commandos in glittering panto dress gleefully romping around on stage like a bunch of youthful thespians, daubed in brightly coloured lipstick, mascara and rouge; add to this a *corps de ballet* with floppy breasts and hobnailed boots, and you have all the ingredients of the annual pantomime performed at the small Barnfield Theatre in Exeter. It is all a great big family affair, with wives and sweethearts joining in the festive antics. For the whole of the 3-week run, including a matinée each Saturday, all the girls – that is, the real girls – become backstage hands. They sew and press torn costumes, help with the make-up, dress the performers and maintain a steady supply of hot refreshments to the 'stars', as well as assisting senior citizens and the handicapped to their seats.

Opening night rivals the première of any West End musical. There are the usual first-night jitters and good-natured leg pulling, accompanied by such theatrical mimicry as 'Break a leg, darling!'. Once on stage, as in the Marines' real-life occupations, there is nothing amateurish about the annual panto; everything is fun and frolic from curtain up to the grand finale. These strapping Marines have them rolling in the aisles with laughter, the children screaming with delight at the antics of Sergeant-Major Gutlumber, billed as 'Snivelling Creep' in the programme, while bewildered grown-ups, unfamiliar with the 'in' jokes, try to crack the humour code. Why is it all so much fun for everyone?

'Because the audience likes to see men of authority make fools of themselves,' says one of the cast.

Marines are renowned for their good-natured self-mockery; after all, to do some of the things they do in real life, without a sense of humour and fun, would be intolerable.

The whole show is a gigantic Marine farce, written, directed, produced and choreographed by members of the Sergeants' mess, with all the usual panto oom-pa-pas and horsey sound effects coming from the resident Marine band at the Lympstone Commando Training Centre (CTCRM). Amid all the hilarity, the pantomime is a serious business for the seniors' mess, and they are justifiably proud that each year they contribute a great deal of money to charity. Everything they make goes to some worthy cause or other. The *Aladdin* panto raised over £25,000 in its 3-week run, and one of the beneficiaries was the Exeter Queen Elizabeth Hospital, which received a heart monitor from some of the proceeds.

If there is a show-stealer it must surely be the 8-man *corps de ballet* dressed in tutus, wigs, socks and Government-issue combat boots. Tripping across the stage to the music of 'Hello Dolly', they give, believe it or not, their own rendition of the cancan.

Mel Walker is a Marine Warrant Officer; he is also the choreographer for the current production, *Aladdin RM*. As anyone in the theatre will tell you, panto can be fun, but it can also be fraught with problems. Our theatrically minded commandos are no different from other actors, and, similar to any military operation, there are problems to be solved. What are they?

'Convincing them that they can do it, and that they are not going to go on stage and look totally stupid in a way that will offend themselves,' says Mel Walker.

How does he manage to persuade his messmates that they should forsake all their spare time and take to the boards for a panto season?

He pauses and smiles – a knowing sort of smile. 'A lot of these guys have not so much been press-ganged, but have had a lot of extra encouragement! The RSMs played a strong part in assisting us to get the people we need! Believe it or not, most of these fellows have never stood on a stage before. We have no theatrical group at Lympstone, so getting a cast is not easy.'

Unlike most theatre folk, Warrant Officer Lionel Oliver is a modest commando impresario, lacking any of the dandified affectations of his professional counterparts. Without him, there just would not be a panto. As with many aspects of military life, he was 'volunteered' for Marine theatricals.

'I was lumbered with this job back in 1980. I have directed seven productions and performed in three others. When I started I didn't have a clue, I really did not have a clue. This is my last. Next year I retire from the Corps.'

What is surprising is that the panto troupe, unlike their sporting counterparts, win no special concessions from the Corps, even though the money they raise goes to charity. Rehearsals are usually held during lunch breaks, and everyone begs and scrounges for props and wardrobe. Since Lionel Oliver took over production, he has progressed from inheriting a £500 loss to handing over a production that is capable of making £30,000, or even more, each year for charity.

In complete contrast to their everyday lives, the Sergeants and Warrant Officers of the seniors' mess produce the annual pantomime. Commando instructors and their colleagues raise thousands of pounds each year for charity.

118

Every night the 303-seat theatre is jam-packed; it is said that tickets for the show are in such demand that the local touts have no difficulty in selling whatever tickets they can obtain.

Aladdin RM is one of those rollicking shows in which everyone is a star. Few West End impresarios have an inkling that each Christmas down in a small Exeter theatre there is one of the funniest, most side-splitting shows to be seen anywhere. For where else would you find such outrageous characters as 'Princess Jasmine, alias Hannah Smell – contrary bit of crumpet'; 'Slave of the Girdle – from Down-Under'; and, best of all, 'Aladdin, the Prince of Twits'?

PART 5

THE LEADERS

THE GENERALS

Lieutenant-General Henry York La Roche Beverley, OBE
Commandant-General, Royal Marines

Few would have thought that the tall, well-suited man picking up the afternoon post on the doormat of a suburban house near the Thames was about to be promoted to the nation's number-one Marine. Tall and athletic-looking, he has a strong, sculptured, weather-beaten face and dark piercing eyes. Only the gently receding hairline suggests that he could be in his early fifties.

Lieutenant-General Beverley has been a Royal Marine for thirty-six years, and is married with two attractive daughters. His wife Sally recalls their first meeting. 'We met in a Chelsea pub along with a group of friends. Henry had just come back from New Zealand and I was working with British Overseas Airways (BOAC) – not flying, I had a ground job. We were married quite quickly. I always remember my mother saying, "Do you know what you are doing?" and I said, "Of course I do." In fact I didn't at all – I hadn't a clue what military life was all about.'

How does she feel about her husband being a high-profile terrorist target?

'It worries me, but I don't think about it.' She pauses before continuing, the attractive, intelligent face belying her concern. 'You get used to it – you take it in your stride.'

She sees her role as helping her husband wherever possible, as she herself does not work now. 'Most of Henry's appointments have involved a lot of entertaining; during our time in Bermuda we held parties in our home for forty, sometimes fifty guests.' Playfully she continues, 'I couldn't do it now, I had youth on my side then. Now that the kitchen is complete we will have kitchen suppers with no more than eight guests – there's no room for more.'

General Beverley was born into a naval family: his father served on HMS *Protector*, *Sussex*, *Resource* and *Cumberland*, in the North Atlantic and the Pacific, leaving the service as a Vice-Admiral. So it was at the early age of five that the General found himself in a Northamptonshire prep school. 'A bit traumatic in many ways,' he recalls.

Then on to Wellington College, and at the age of eighteen he embarked on his Marine career. Though educated at one of Britain's top public schools, the General tends to favour the philosophy of comprehensive education these days, though he is quick to point out that as far as the Royal Marines are concerned, they are not biased towards any one sector when it comes to officer selection.

'As you go around the Corps,' he says, 'you will find that we are a very middle-class organization, and it is difficult to identify those who went to a public school or attended the maintained sector.'

The General's military career has followed a pattern similar to that of several of his contemporaries: early years in overseas postings, in his case Malta, Cyprus, New Zealand, the West Indies and the United States. After being on the staff of the Army Staff College at Camberley, he went on to command 42 Commando and to serve in Northern Ireland – for which he was awarded the Order of the British Empire – later becoming Commandant of the Commando Training Centre and ADC to Her Majesty the Queen. Subsequently he commanded 3 Commando Brigade before being promoted to Major-General in 1986. He was appointed Commandant-General in June 1990.

Mention Marine standards and General Beverley is adamant that they are better than they ever were. 'I believe that the standards required for our officers and recruits are far higher than ever before; our training is far more objective and it is administered by particularly professional people.'

He is also a realist. 'We have always got to justify ourselves and I don't believe we have any difficulty in doing that. I would challenge anybody to tell me a more cost-effective organization in the British Armed Forces than the Royal Marines, considering the variety of specialist roles which we fulfil. In broad terms, we represent one and a half per cent of the naval budget. Our equipment is not highly sophisticated, nor very expensive.'

He stretches his long legs and pauses to reflect. 'The Marines are remarkably adaptable. From being the twilight-of-the-Empire bushfire-type force, going to every confrontation around the world that British Forces have been involved in, from the Yangtze, Palestine and Aden, to being a potent flexible force ready to defend the flanks of NATO against the Soviet threat.'

Perhaps his views on past military leaders reveal more of him than anything else. 'In war you need the mix of the unconventional, like Wingate and Stirling, with the others, but in the end the bread-and-butter victories are won by your Montgomerys and Slims.'

Does he feel threatened as a terrorist target?

'I don't see myself being significantly more at threat than soldiers in places like Mill Hill or Turnhill Barracks. It's a fact of life in the services that everybody has got to be vigilant at all times to the threat that confronts them. After taking all the precautions that you possibly can, the bottom line is that you cannot allow yourself to get into a state of total neurosis about it. You cannot live in a cage all your life. You have to be sensible, get on and do your job and live your life.'

Lieutenant-General Sir Martin Garrod, KCB, OBE
Commandant-General, Royal Marines
(retired 1990)

The General lives in a tiled red-brick house surrounded by garden in a quiet corner of a London suburb with his wife Jill and, apart from the usual round of official functions and the occasional dinner party at home, the General and his wife love the quiet retreat of their garden and comfy home. Tall and distinguished, the General has none of the usual pompous mannerisms of high military rank; he exudes the tranquillity of the cleric or the contemplative academic.

Reminiscing on his youth he says, 'I was born in Darjeeling and spent the first ten years of my life in India. My father was a Church of England vicar, and consequently we moved a great deal. I went to a mixed school in Naini Tal, so got to know the Indians extremely well. When I came to England I spent a short time at Christ Church Cathedral Choir School – not as a chorister, I was too old by then – before going to Sherborne.'

He goes on, 'Yes, I'm an advocate of the public school system. I gained a great deal from it and still retain some very close friends from those years. I enjoyed it, though I know not everyone did.'

Lady Garrod is his constant companion and travels with him whenever possible, whether it is to the terror-ridden streets of Northern Ireland or some far-off contingent of Marines operating in the South China Sea. They both look affectionately at each other as they recall with youthful delight how they first met on a blind date at a Summer Ball, when the General was serving as housemaster at the Royal Marines' School of Music. Both their families are steeped in several generations of Marine tradition: Lady Garrod's father was killed on the Dieppe Raid when she was only four months old. 'Mother was left very badly off after the war with two small children to care for,' she recalls.

Does the Corps get one and a half for the price of one? The General believes they get two, but Lady Garrod does not see it that way. She is a handsome women with a ticklish sense of humour.

'Honestly I don't look at it like that. I am a three-generation Royal Marine, for a start, and I love the Corps. Grandpa joined in 1898; it's a way of life. Martin and I do as much as we can together – we always have done. We can come back from a function and say, "Do you know what so and so said?" and we can talk about it.' She gestures to her husband. 'Teamwork, isn't it, darling?' He nods and replies, 'Absolutely.'

With that touch of elegance reminiscent of the 1920s, she lights a finger-slim cheroot and continues, 'It's much more interesting than most jobs people have. I went off to Northern Ireland with Martin for eight months and it was one of the best things I did in my life. I grew up, I think.'

Their day begins at six o'clock with the General making the morning tea. Rarely do they have a weekend free from the obligatory military rounds. Entertaining at home is limited to a dozen guests, with the usual mix of military attachés, senior civil servants and a coterie of service bigwigs. Now that their children are following their own careers, Lady Garrod works two days a week at the Royal College of Heralds, which she regards as more of a passion than a job; even so, she manages with a minimal two staff.

'My dear, it's all very peaceful,' she remarks with a touch of worldly wisdom. 'I am a great believer in the less people you have, the fewer the problems.'

Unlike some military figures, General Garrod has not surrounded himself with layers of military memorabilia: their home, the twenty-sixth in twenty-six years, is comfortable and welcoming, with snug easy-chairs, family etchings and tranquil watercolours on the walls. A keen photographer, the General has two Impressionist-style photographs of his daughters on a small corner table; their bookshelves contain works by Hardy, Manning, Susan Crossland, Rushdie and Forster.

General Garrod received his commission in 1953, and on completion of his training was assigned to 40 Commando in Malta as a Rifle Troop Subaltern. He went on to serve in Cyprus, Malaya and Borneo, with a home tour of duty with the Royal Marines' School of Music. After attending the Army Staff College at Camberley, he returned to Malaya and in 1969 was appointed to Headquarters Far East Land Forces in Singapore.

After several tours of Northern Ireland, where he was mentioned in dispatches and awarded the Order of the British Empire (OBE), he was promoted to Colonel and appointed to the Commandant-General's office in London. In September 1983, with the rank of Brigadier, he was appointed Aide-de-Camp to Her Majesty the Queen, and the following year was promoted to Major-General and appointed Chief of Staff to the Commandant, Royal Marines. On 8 May 1987 he became the nation's number-one Marine on his appointment as Commandant-General of the Royal Marines. He received his knighthood (KCB) the following year.

Looking towards the horizon of the twenty-first century, General Garrod is convinced that the Royal Marines are in good shape, though he willingly admits that there have been times when the Marines have had their backs to the wall, in respect of their own future. As he sees it, all that is past. But there are fresh problems.

'If there are two things that keep me awake at night they are amphibious ships and manpower,' he confesses. To have an effective amphibious force the General knows he must get his replacement ships on schedule. Then there is the nagging matter of retention – keeping his highly trained Marines in the service.

'The Corps is up to strength, but we are having to run hard to keep fully manned.' General Garrod is a realist and knows he has a problem. 'Over the past year one has noticed a significant increase in trained wastage. Our high-calibre young men feel that after five or six years they have a green beret, they've done a couple of tours in Northern Ireland and learnt to ski in Norway, so they want to try something else. There's no dissatisfaction with the Corps. It's more a perception that the grass may be greener on the other side. It's also a reflection on society. Young people are moving about far more than they ever did in the past.'

Major-General Robin J. Ross, OBE
Major-General Commando Forces, Royal Marines

When we met, Major-General Ross had a secluded office in the delightfully rustic old Eastney Barracks, near Portsmouth in Hampshire. There is a quiet, cloistered feel about the old seaward-looking Victorian buildings with their long, regimented lines of windows and quaint turreted walls. His office is large, bright and airy, with none of the accoutrements of high military office, its uncluttered appearance indicating that the inhabitant has simple tastes.

The General is wearing what Marines call half-lovats – khaki shirt with scarlet rank tabs and olive-green barathea trousers with a broad belt in the Corps' colours. He has a strong determined face with an underlying sensitive quality, revealing a delicate sense of kindness and understanding. He exudes that rare quality of being a natural leader, which is no doubt one of the reasons he is so popular with his staff. Out of uniform you might think he was a schoolmaster or in medicine. His father was in the Marines at a time when the Navy carried several hundred Marines on each of her big ships.

'Like so many of my generation I never really knew my father, being born a few weeks after war was declared. I remember the first time I saw him I was terrified,' he recalls. 'He was too old for commando service, but was involved in special operations in the Far East. After the war he served for another ten years and retired as a Lieutenant-Colonel.'

Like many others, General Ross chose his father's service and joined the Marines after leaving Wellington, just before his eighteenth birthday. 'In my day at Wellington, unless you were very bright, you were not encouraged to go to university. It was a question of which bit of the service you were going into, if you were not going into the Army.'

As a young Marine officer he managed to see a great deal of the world: North Africa, Malta, Aden, with 45 Commando, and later Singapore with 40 Commando. He was in his early forties when he went up to Corpus Christi College, Cambridge, where he read for an M. Phil. in International Relations. Five years later he was appointed Aide-de-Camp to Her Majesty the Queen, and in 1988 was promoted to Major-General. General Ross is a man with definite innovative ideas, unlike most senior military figures, who tend to toe the regimental line.

On the Corps' relations with the media he says, 'I think we have tended to regard anybody who looks at us too closely as being a potential enemy. But I think we learnt during the Falklands War that an open-minded attitude, to people who are genuinely interested in what you are doing, is the only

way it can work. If you have a newspaper man, or some other media man, who is clearly anti, then it's never going to work at all. If he's clearly sympathetic, then it seems to be a nonsense not to co-operate fully, and to trust him and allow him to examine your organization, warts and all. We have nothing to be afraid of allowing that to happen these days.'

As one senior NCO on his staff remarked, 'He's a man's man. He's out there in the morning running with his dog, Kate, just like the lads.'

For a senior officer, some of his ideas might be thought heretical in some Marine circles. Consider his opinions on women in the Corps, which he emphasizes is a personal opinion and by no means an *ex-cathedra* statement from his position as General of Marines. 'I believe that we do not make the best use of women in the Corps, and we could do better. I think we are in danger of dragging our heels if we don't get on with it.'

He was choosing his words with care, though there was just the faint hint of a smile on his face as he continued, 'I think we can offer some very challenging, interesting and relevant employment for girls within the Corps, without them having to be part of the WRNS. Personally, I would like to see women employed directly in the Corps. Clearly one has to be sensible about this, for there are certain jobs which it would be impractical for them to do. I would not in any sense envisage girls in the front line – by that I mean clutching rifles and charging up hills in the face of the enemy. This has been tried by the Israelis and been seen to fail. There are all kinds of jobs for them where they could be extremely valuable, working in intelligence, communications, yes, and even flying helicopters.'

How about women one day wearing the green beret?

'I see no reason why there could not be a modified green beret course for girl entrants. You could design a course which could be as testing in both psychological and physical terms, but tailored to meet the different capabilities of the female.' Convinced that women Marines would be a great asset to the Corps, he expands his beliefs further. 'Many girls and women I know have considerably greater psychological stamina than men do. I have never thought of the idea of a man going through the business of giving birth – but I suspect he would not be very good at it!'

One gets the feeling that General Robin Jeremy Ross is something of a romantic. Certainly a lateral thinker, a modest individualist. Even the most ardent anti-militarist or CND activist could not be offended by this quiet, unassuming warrior.

Major-General Nicholas Francis Vaux, CB, DSO
Major-General Commando Forces, Royal Marines
(retired June 1990)

As the old frontiers of Europe dissolve before our eyes, and the risks of confrontation with Communist forces seem less of an apocalyptic nightmare, combat-experienced Generals are becoming increasingly rare. General Nick Vaux is a Falklands veteran. In the closing days of the Falklands War, defying sniper fire, along with his Marines of 42 Commando, he fought his way through the rocky crags of Mount Harriet against fiercely defended Argentinian positions. For renowned and gallant service he received the Distinguished Service Order (DSO).

There is nothing flashy or ostentatious about Nick Vaux; behind the tough, stalwart face and stocky frame he can be quiet, shy and retiring. So perhaps it is his love of horses – he is an inter-service equestrian – and of the outdoors that can tell us most about the soft-spoken General who led his Marines to victory in the South Atlantic.

'If you find yourself in a minefield you must go on,' he said to his troops on the eve of the night attack to take Mount Harriet. 'However great the temptation, you must not stop for your "oppos". You must go on and finish the attack, or it will cost more lives in the end.'

His Marine career has followed the familiar path of many senior officers: troop and company commander, Army Staff College, a posting to the United States Marine Corps, then the College of Defence Studies, and Chief of Staff at Commando Forces Headquarters. In 1987 he was promoted to Major-General Royal Marines.

General Vaux, though quiet of manner, is an outspoken man and shows grave concern regarding the Corps' ageing equipment. 'There is a sense of frustration about the deficiencies and the quality of equipment that we actually have. We haven't got enough vehicles in Commando Forces to tactically achieve the kind of operational task that we ought to, and we are increasingly working with technology that is either outdated or simply deteriorating. Communications is a typical example. Our communications are old, outdated, and they don't work.'

For the past few days the General has been in the field with his Marines, overseeing 'Rolling Deep', one of the many annual exercises in which the Corps is involved. He is weary, rather than tired. The austere surroundings of the dilapidated army camp on bleak Salisbury Plain, where we met, do little to alleviate the facts. The operational capability of the world's foremost commando force is being jeopardized by inferior equipment. For the Marines who yomped their way across the east

Falklands and fought such a gallant campaign, these must seem disconsolate times, regardless of their professional loyalties.

'I think you get what you pay for.' The General continues, 'If the nation wants 3 Commando Brigade or Commando Forces to go to war at a moment's notice, like they did in the Falklands, you really have to provide them with the best kit, and I think a lot of people do feel that perhaps this is no longer so. They are disillusioned.'

General Vaux also suggests that service pay has not kept pace with inflation; consequently, increasing numbers are leaving the Corps. 'Our Marines are intelligent chaps, who make comparisons to see what they can earn in other services, or in the police. The police are one of the greatest drains on the Royal Marines. The other factor is the turmoil. We have a very intensive programme, and most of Commando Forces go to Norway every winter. Every other year we go to Northern Ireland, and on top of this we have our annual round of exercises, like this one. The young thoroughly enjoy it, that is what they join for. But if you are married, as a Corporal, Sergeant or Lieutenant, and you have a young family and a wife who wants to see something of you, in the end she, or you yourself, will conclude that this is not tolerable.'

When questioned about the future of the Royal Marines the General thinks carefully for a few moments, while staring out of the window of the cheerless barrack blocks watching the fading afternoon light.

He sums it up this way. 'I think this is a critical time because at the present moment this Government is making up its mind whether it can afford to pay for maintaining the amphibious capability, and that means buying new ships. We have to have a commando carrier. No matter how many helicopters you have, we won't be able to carry out the tactical envelopment without a flight deck. One of the great fallacies is that you can have the specialist ships, but not a specialist amphibious Corps. You can't just pick up a battalion of Gurkhas and put them in a ship, because it doesn't work. If we decide, for whatever reasons, not to replace the amphibious shipping, then yes, I will be very concerned about our future. I genuinely believe that all the planning and staffing and consensus over the past few years in the MoD will persuade ministers that they must pay for the new amphibious ships, and if they do, well then, that guarantees the future of the Royal Marines well into the twenty-first century. My own feeling at the moment is that ministers have accepted the idea.'

The Officers

Previous page: At a dinner to commemorate the Falklands landings, silver estimated to be worth many thousands of pounds adorns the tables of the Royal Marines' officers' mess in Plymouth, Devon. Mess staff may take a day preparing the silver and setting the tables, before each function.

There was a time – but a few score years ago – when the not too bright offspring of Britain's so-called gentry found their way into three areas of influence in our land: politics; the Church; and what was loosely called 'The Regiment'. For whatever reason, the Navy was never considered to be an alternative, for it was fraught with hardship and uncertainty, even for officers. When the skies too became a battlefield, flying was thought to be a black art and left to the foolish and carefree. After all, being with a sound regiment that displayed a pedigree similar to one's own was surely what mattered most. Connections, money, the right school, together with lisping accents and effete mannerisms were the basic ingredients for young men about to be funnelled into the posh regiments of the nation. The tribalistic aristocracy adopted hallowed rituals: son followed father, who had followed his father; brother beckoned brother; and regimental talent scouts scanned the better families for the new-born male who was still asleep in the cradle. Eton, Harrow, Wellington and a host of other, so-called noble schools of the realm were regularly canvassed for likely military leaders.

Élitism still pervades Britain's military – only a fool would deny it – but the outmoded customs are slipping away: commissions are no longer purchased, while family connections will now guarantee right of passage only into the Household Brigade or some snooty regiment north of the border. And another thing. Regiments no longer have the 'pull' they once enjoyed. Possessing a good science degree from a red-brick university is preferred to knowing the right Chablis to tipple on ladies' night. Besides, these days young men are reticent about committing themselves to a long-term mili-

'You should be on better terms with your razor in the morning, Sir' might well have been the comment to this trainee officer from his NCO instructor at the morning parade. As a deterrent, poorly shaved officers on the training course can be made to shave in public, on the parade square.

tary career. Where once the 'blue-chip' regiments commanded a young man's attention, it is now to the Corps that they are flocking. With Sandhurst on the curriculum vitae, a moderate degree, and four years in the Signals or Engineers, such officers have more to offer private enterprise than time spent as a foot-slogging soldier, no matter how glossy the regiment.

By the very nature of their job, the down-to-earth, no-nonsense bunch of officers in Her Majesty's Royal Marines have few of the tribal characteristics of some military bodies. Conformity is at its least noticeable, fraternalism is preferred to gung-ho militarism, flamboyance is frowned upon, while strutting around peacock-like is considered best left to the Guards, Yanks and the banana republics.

As one young 23-year-old Marine officer recalls,

'I was in the company of some Guards officers on a recent Northern Ireland tour; for want of a better word, they were a lot of Yuppies; Fulham Road, Chelsea, that sort of area – they had a lot of problems relating to their men, and were so detached from their troops that they had no idea how they lived. We couldn't treat our Marines like that.'

Most in the Corps would agree that élitism has, by and large, been fed into the military shredder. Batmen, along with other forms of ritual snobbery, have for the most part disappeared, though some will confess that there is a gentle whiff of boorish superiority among many of the middle-ranking officers courting the cocktail circuit, hell-bent on hobnobbing their way to the top.

Marines of all ranks quietly revel in their Janus-like personalities. Officially they are sea soldiers and, in the American idiom, 'kissing cousins' of the

135

Navy. Disciplinary matters are a question of where you are at the time; however, if naval rules do not apply, then to be sure the Army Act will. But the Marines generally use their dual nature to their own advantage: if they do not like the Navy way of doing things, they will with one accord claim Army status. Similarly, should they disagree with some part of their Army role, they will take refuge within the maritime fold. All of them, from Bootneck to General, have learnt to play the system to their own advantage.

It may rankle with the Royal Military Academy, Sandhurst and those other hallowed institutions of officer training – the naval colleges of Greenwich and Dartmouth – that Britain's Royal Marines prefer to do things differently and train their Marine officers alongside recruits. Undoubtedly this is considered anathema in certain stuffy officer circles, where it is still believed that the troops should not be privy to seeing their future leaders making asses of themselves while training. The Marine hierarchy, on the other hand, is unrepentant and quick to defend the method and its principles: rightly or wrongly, the Marines believe that training their recruits and officers alongside each other helps to tie the knot of lasting comradeship. No doubt the system has its merits, and helps to sustain the 'family' ethic. However, some trainees think otherwise, and will tell you that their main concern at Lympstone is getting through the course and obtaining that tantalizing accolade – the green beret. Other than that, it is generally believed by trainees that the Marine establishment is deceiving itself if it believes there is any prevailing virtue in the Lympstone system of combined officer and recruit training. As one former Marine says, 'You see so little of each other anyway, I really can't see what benefits there are. All you think about is passing out and forgetting Lympstone.'

The officer selection process is a rigorous and painstaking one. At an estimated cost of £1,000 per week for each officer during training, it has to be. Each applicant is invited to attend a three-day Potential Officers Course (POC) at the Commando Training Centre (CTC) at Lympstone, followed later by another screening process by the Admiralty Interview Board (AIB) at HMS *Sultan*, a shore-based naval establishment at Gosport in Hampshire. Brawn alone will not impress the selectors. Modern warfare demands a mental ability that can function under stress, along with a combination of leadership and communication skills, which enable the young officer to impart his intentions with decisive clarity.

Previous page: Amid the luxurious surroundings of the officers' mess at Plymouth, Marines who took part in the Falklands operation gather each year with their guests to commemorate the landing at San Carlos Water. In the early hours of the morning, at the time when the troops waded ashore, the event is toasted in vintage wines and champagne. By candlelight the Marines and their guests dine on a menu of Patagonian crested teal pâté, Chartres river trout and roast rack of lamb while listening to music from a Marine orchestra.

While the Army trains all its potential officers at Sandhurst, and the Navy and the Air Force have similar institutions, the Royal Marines prefer to train their own officers and Marines at the Commando Training Centre, at Lympstone in Devon.

As for all graduating students the age-old rituals are followed, and the moment is preserved for the family.

'Being a smooth talker will not get you through the AIB. You've got to know your stuff,' one young Marine officer confided. Training officers at Lympstone will admit that the system is not foolproof, and they are cagey about their failure rates, but are satisfied that during the few days the candidate spends with them, as part of the selection process, they manage to weed out those lacking the necessary flair and zest. Regarding their failures and misfits, they prefer their 'gentlemen' to find out for themselves when Marine life is not to their liking, rather than give the 'family' the embarrassment of telling them they have no future in the Corps.

'When I joined the Corps twenty-three years ago, I hadn't a clue what I was getting into,' confesses one of the officers who is now responsible for training the younger generation. Times have changed. In the intervening years, training costs have obviously made the Marines far more circumspect in their selection process.

'There are few born leaders,' the officer in charge of training points out. 'What we try to do here is to teach it. A man has to make the best of his personal qualities.'

As a yardstick he sets out the three fundamental requirements for an officer candidate: leadership, physical abilities and communication skills. He continues with his slick, well-rehearsed patter, 'I need a guy who has a robust mental faculty, because I am going to throw at him a lot of information and he will have to apply it under stressful situations – under pressure – because that's what war is about. On the physical side I am a firm believer that if we can get a committed guy with an arm and a leg in each corner through the gate, we will get him through. What I am trying to produce is a military professional who is an excellent man manager as well.'

Young Marine Lieutenants, unlike their counterparts in other services, receive their commission on entering the Marines. They are also trained by the finest NCOs in the Corps and by personally selected officers. For the most part, the officers' course is similar to that of Marine recruits, but more intensive and six months longer. Life on the upper floors of the officers' mess at Lympstone, where the newly minted Lieutenants live, resembles the senior year of a public school, rather than a hard-hitting military training institution. Radios blare out the popular tunes of the day, towelled bodies pore over maps, ribald laughter echoes along the corridors, piles of military webbing and footwear litter doorways. A West African, over in England to be trained with the Marines, lies exhausted from the day's activities on the floor of his room, gazing motionless at the ceiling. In the dining room below, attractive waitresses in neat black dresses and pretty white pinnies set out the silver for lunch.

It is a crisp morning in July on a remote part of Dartmoor known as Cross Furzes. The mist is thinning, revealing the green and brown of the rugged countryside. Above, through the broken stratus clouds, the sky is a milky blue. In a corner of a field a crude table has been set out, and on it a collection of green berets, each with a name on the inside. A young Chinese Lieutenant from Singapore, training with the Marines, has thoughtfully placed a small bunch of wild flowers in a simple jar on the table. On another table, near the hedge, is an empty silver bowl from the officers' mess, soon to be filled with a mixture of Pimms and lemonade. Major-General Nick Vaux, who will present the green berets, chats with everyone, moving easily among the assembled officers and NCOs who are part of the training team.

At the other end of Dartmoor there is great excitement among a group of young Marine Lieutenants about to embark on their final test for the green beret. Taut with expectation, and longing to be off, few of them have slept through the night. Into the late hours the 4- and 5-man syndicates were making their final plans. Their route is unknown and fearsome; equipment is checked for the umpteenth time, feet are pampered with powder and extra socks, water bottles are filled, radios tested, compasses and maps secured. Nothing is left to chance.

Before the arrival of the pencil-thin, slate-grey dawn, the young officers, barely twenty years old, slip out into the velvet blackness of the moor in full battle order at the beginning of the dreaded '30-miler'. They have eight hours to reach their objective – Cross Furzes.

Lieutenant Jason Ward knows when he sets out that he is going to have trouble, so he takes his turn to carry the radio on the first leg. His syndicate sets out at a brisk pace with everyone in high spirits. This is the 'big one', the culmination of a year's hard training. Everyone has agreed that they must cover as many miles as possible before the sun comes up.

By the third hour Jason Ward's legs are beginning to feel the strain and he is already flagging – he keeps reminding himself that he must not delay the others, but his companions never leave him far behind. How his muscles ache! His feet are now swollen and blistered. He wills the pain to go away. He has heard others say how there is always a bad spot during the march, but that it will pass. 'You will walk yourself through it,' they say. As the sun comes up he welcomes its warmth on his tired body. From time to time one of his companions falls behind and walks with him, willing him on. At the halfway mark his condition is serious. The doctor tells him that he should not continue, for his feet are badly blistered and he is near exhaustion. But Jason Ward is adamant. He is going to finish. Mile after weary mile he struggles on. Every so often someone keeps him company; on one occasion he recalls that it is one of the officers from the training team, encouraging and cajoling. Inevitably everyone out on the moor is willing him on. Time and distance are meaningless. For Jason it is a question of putting one foot in front of the other. How he keeps going neither he nor his friends can tell; everyone agrees that it is due to his dogged will to complete the course. The last few miles are agonizing. His companions see him coming down the road and they run out to help. Exhausted and limping, he drags his weary body to the finishing point; his eyes are glazed and there are trickles of mucus oozing from his nose. Saliva trickles from his mouth. They lay him on the grass, where a medical orderly tends his blistered feet. He has finished the course. For Jason Ward, that is all that matters.

To outsiders, Lieutenant Ward might well be considered foolhardy, but to others what he did is understandable. It represents the singular spirit of determination with which all Marines are imbued.

THE NCOS

As any old Navy hand will tell you there is a great deal of conventional wisdom in the adage that if you care to know what's happening aboard any of HM ships, make your way to the Petty Officers' mess. It is no different in the Marines. If you want to confirm recent gossip or scandal, then a well-placed pint in the Sergeants' mess works wonders.

An NCO in the Royal Marines holds a very special place within the Corps: he is the hub in the wheel of command, the conduit and the lubricant which make the Corps hum with sparkling efficiency. Unlike his American counterpart, he does not project that over-creased, sanitized look. That is not the 'Royals'' style. He is spruce rather than flash. Nor is he necessarily over-strapping or full of swank. Though he can be all of these when the need arises.

Marine NCOs are expected to undertake far more responsibility than NCOs in the other Armed Forces. Promotion can be demoralizingly slow in coming – four years at least to make Corporal. To earn a place in the plusher surrounds of the Sergeants' mess could mean a further three years, while few will be promoted to Colour Sergeant in less than twelve. Most Warrant Officers could patiently wait seventeen years to obtain that treasured title, 'Mr so and so'.

Any outsider could be forgiven for concluding that the spirit of the Corps is bound up within its seniors; unlike their Guards counterparts, with their stentorian wails and burlesque mannerisms, they are neither overtly thuggish nor overbearing. They have a quieter stamp of authority, more subtle, well-controlled, even refined. This has not always been the case: there were times when Corporals and Sergeants struck terror in the hearts of Marines, and when even the slightest misdemeanour was punishable by confinement to barracks or imprisonment in some rigorous 'brig' (military prison).

As might be expected, there are sharp divisions between the NCOs' and officers' messes. Even in the egalitarian-minded Marines, the age-old caste system prevails. The 'them and us' is plainly evident. In the event of a senior NCO deciding to take a commission, he is never expected to return to the NCOs' mess. Even an invitation from former colleagues is regarded with disapproval, for the mess now regards him as being 'one of them' and he has abrogated his right of return.

During the arduous '30-miler' officers and instructors join in to give moral support, while some NCOs finish barely conscious of their surroundings.

Certain NCOs are blatantly outspoken concerning the quality of young officers entering the Corps today and are none too polite about their superiors.

'They come into the Corps with their fancy education and acquired accents and think they know it all. Most of them are too bloody arrogant and opinionated for their own good,' says one of the seniors involved in the training process.

This is not an isolated observation, but a recurring comment made by a cross-section of people in and outside the Marines, who come into contact with junior and middle-ranking officers. Call it immaturity, a failure to communicate or, simply, bad manners – the system absorbs it, and the Corps soldiers on its own indomitable way.

It is a well-known fact that a young officer is as good as the NCOs who trained him. As the Corps prides itself on being the world's finest, NCOs at Lympstone are mindful that they are responsible for training a pre-eminent military leader. Those who malinger and continually fail to meet the required standards are admonished in no uncertain terms.

A former Lympstone instructor, exasperated by the poor performance of one of his young trainee officers, takes him aside to somewhere they will not be disturbed.

'Lieutenant Smith [it is not his true name], take those pips from your shoulder, Sir. Forget my stripes, Sir, I am now talking to you man-to-man. You, Sir, are one big fuck-up from beginning to

In an open field on the edge of Dartmoor, following their completion of the '30-miler', fledgeling officers, all in their early twenties, receive their green berets. Blistered feet have been tended by medical orderlies, while a bunch of wild flowers has been placed on a table surrounded by the hard-won berets. They are nearing the end of their training. Within a few months some of them could be leading a section of Marines through the streets of West Belfast; others could be assigned to a Commando that is about to commence its Arctic training in northern Norway. Regardless of the steady stream of young men being accepted for Marine officer training, there is an ever-increasing number of highly experienced officers resigning their commissions, knowing that, with defence cutbacks, they are rank-frozen, and realizing there is no future with the Corps.

end. You're continually screwing up, Sir. Pull your bloody finger out, man, or I'll see that you are a civvy in no time at all.'

Within a very short time the young Lieutenant has resigned his commission. From the NCOs' point of view, the Royal Marines are better off without him.

'Take it from me,' confides a Warrant Officer in the Sergeants' mess, 'look around you, this is where it happens – we run the bloody show.' This is not a chance remark gleaned from the Sergeants' mess bar, but the general opinion of most of the Corps' NCOs.

'Sergeant-power' is strongly denied by the officers, who put it down to fanciful thinking, the mischievous media, and a few disgruntled old

sweats. One senior officer makes this comment, 'Some seniors may think they run the Corps – but I have the ultimate say!'

Another officer, a young Lieutenant, is more forthright and admits that so-called 'Sergeant-power' and all that it implies undoubtedly does exist within the Corps. There is no question that the debate will continue – officers claiming that their NCOs are the world's finest, yet underlining that it is they who are firmly in command.

While the Marine hierarchy will passionately deny the existence of 'Sergeant-power', its NCOs will dutifully observe the daily rituals, calling the officers 'Sir', but knowing full well they are the co-hesive element, the indispensable link in the chain; in effect, the unrivalled authority within the Corps.

AFTER THE CORPS

Bill Sparks

Marines the world over, be they British, American, Dutch or the many others serving in the forces of the Western powers, all regard themselves as being part of one large 'family'. Undoubtedly there is something about being a Marine than appeals to the tribalism in man. No Marines are more family-oriented than the Royal Marines. Regardless of their low profile, on leaving the Corps they have filtered into all areas of society, and not only into the obvious niches like the police, fire service and the security industry. After leaving the Corps, Marines have entered the priesthood, been elected to Parliament, become stuntmen and pilots for Arabian princes.

One ex-Marine is currently a Yeoman Warder at the Tower of London; a former Captain is with a financial house in Hong Kong; while another young Marine, a Falklands veteran, works in the building trade. There are over a score of former Marines of varying ranks employed in the House of Commons and the House of Lords, a place where ex-Guardsmen once revelled in their monopoly of power. Compared to the Guards, who conjure their way into positions of privilege and high office, Marines are in general neither dilettante nor snobbish. Though many wear the Corps' tie with pride, ex-Marines are not in the habit of believing that this guarantees their right of entry into the better clubs in town. As Marines, they will 'yomp' their way to success, for the 'Royals' have little regard for the caste or privilege ethic.

Four of these ex-Marines tell their stories. In their various ways all have been successful after leaving the Corps but, as it is in life, some more so than others.

Bill Sparks, DSM
Retired

In a remote enclave of neatly groomed mobile bungalows in the heart of the lush Sussex countryside lives the lone survivor of one of the greatest military escapades of the century. Inside the neat, welcoming home a few mementoes remain from the old days: photos, plaques and an old service identification tag. You will, however, find no veteran's medals. Sadly these had to be sold to keep a roof over this old campaigner's head.

Remember 'The Cockleshell Heroes'? These men were not the imaginary wafer-thin dare-devils conceived by some Hollywood hack. Far from it. Their daring mission – some might say foolhardy – was as bold and courageous as any to come out of the war. For his courage and enterprise Corporal 'Bill' Sparks, Royal Marines, was decorated with the Distinguished Service Medal (DSM) for his part in what was officially known as 'Operation Frankton'.

The well-known story of the Cockleshell Heroes has been recorded in books and on film, and is recognized worldwide as one of the most audacious clandestine operations of the Second World War. Ten Marines, teamed in 2-man crews, set out in five small kayak-type canoes, after being launched from a submarine near the French coast, and paddled over 100 miles up the Gironde River to Bordeaux to destroy enemy shipping with limpet mines. Such a suicidal mission was fraught with hazards and uncertainties, and it is hardly surprising that only four of the Marines, in two canoes, penetrated the target area. Only two of the team survived – Major 'Blondie' Hasler, who conceived the raid, and the lively outspoken Cockney from around the Angel, Islington, Bill Sparks.

You could not have a finer friend than Bill Sparks. He came from a generation of East End Londoners whose daily life revolved around the concepts of loyalty, generosity and comradeship. For many, it was all they had to give during the Depression years of the 1920s. Bill is no griper, but all is not well these days between Bill and the Corps he so faithfully served. 'It's all because I auctioned my medals,' he confides. 'There was a time when I would be asked to talk to the young officers coming into the Corps, but not any more.' Even though he is reluctant to say it in so many words, Bill Sparks, one of this nation's heroes, feels that he and his former comrades are being swept under the mat by certain factions within the Marines.

In a re-enactment in February 1989 of 'Operation Frankton', the heroic Cockleshell Heroes' raid on Bordeaux harbour, Bill Sparks was neither consulted nor asked to accompany the Marine party. 'I would have loved to have met up with René Flaud and the Maudinaud brothers, who helped "Blondie" and me escape, and to have been given the opportunity of visiting the area again, but I was not invited.'

Bill came from a poor family. 'Two up and two down, shared by two families, the "cazi" was out the back; we had a large copper to do the washing in, and there was no lino on the floor. We used to bath in a large wooden bath out the back' – this is the way Bill describes his home surroundings. 'We had a very rough time. When my dad came out of the Navy he was years and years without a job. Just couldn't find one. We were on the breadline.'

Within two months of the outbreak of war Bill Sparks had enlisted in the Marines, and found himself in the old Deal barracks with nine months of training to endure – gravel-bashing, as it was known in his day.

'I drew five shillings signing-on money, and when we arrived at Deal they gave us another five shillings,' Bill recalls. 'I thought, this is all right, until I realized that it was an advance on my week's pay. In those days you got fourteen shillings a week: beer was fivepence a pint and a packet of five Woodbines cost twopence. I used to smoke ten a day.'

Bill Sparks will tell you that he had a good war. As a member of a Special Forces Unit, he found himself involved in all kinds of skulduggery, which suited the cheerful Cockney's character. He managed to survive the war when many of his comrades did not. Promotion eluded him, for he was too soft-hearted and easy-going. 'The Commanding Officer expected me to report my mates.' Bill could not do that, and his forthright, independent spirit deprived him of advancement.

Men like Bill Sparks never see themselves as heroes. Most will tell you they were trained to do a job and they did it to the best of their ability. Heroes are like that.

'I didn't think I deserved the medal,' he says without any false modesty. 'It cost eight of the finest lives that could have been brought on earth and I got the award.' Sadness shows in his pale, ageing face as he speaks. He pauses momentarily, no doubt casting his mind back over the intervening years. 'What annoys me is that these lads who gave their lives received nothing and that really hurt me. The only posthumous awards were two MIDs (Mentioned in Dispatches), which were for the two other lads that got into the target area with us.'

After the war Bill Sparks vowed that his nine comrades would never be forgotten. After thirty-eight years of campaigning, he succeeded in having a memorial dedicated to those whom the world knows as 'The Cockleshell Heroes'. It is a simple monument of stone situated close to the sea on the Dorset coast. Along with the names of those that took part, an inscription reads:

Of the many brave and dashing raids carried out by the men of Combined Operations Command, none was more courageous or imaginative than 'Operation Frankton'
Mountbatten of Burma

Just as war brings its devastation and hardship, all too frequently the aftermath of war is no better.

Governments and politicians forget, families stifle their tears, and heroes are expected to fade gently away. After the war, like his father before him, times were hard for Bill Sparks. Jobs came and went: bus driver; police Lieutenant in Malaya; labourer on building sites; Christmas postman; insurance agent and shoe repairer. After years of dead-end job-hunting, his fortunes finally changed and he found his way into London Transport, retiring as a bus inspector.

When Bill's pension was cut by twenty pounds a week he knew he was in trouble, for he stood to lose the cosy £72,000 home he and his second wife Rene had retired to in the Sussex countryside. He knew his medals were worth money. An old friend from his service days had told him they were worth at least £20,000. There was nothing else for it – the medals had to be sold to keep a roof over their heads.

There was a feeling in certain Marine quarters that Bill's collection of medals should be given to the Marines Museum at Eastney. Bill did not see it that way. His hard-won medals were his to do with as he wished. As he explained later, 'Some years ago I was asked if I would bequeath them to the museum. I said no, I'm afraid not. I know the Corps didn't like me selling the medals, but selling them saved my home. Now I don't have to work for the rest of my life.'

Understandably there was a great deal of bickering and consternation on the Marine grapevine, when it became known that Bill's medals were to be auctioned at Sotheby's. An ex-Marine Major turned up on Bill's doorstep, confident that his £11,000 bid would not be refused. He departed empty-handed, for the canny Eastender knew that it was a paltry offer and that his DSM would fetch far more at auction.

On Thursday, 30 June 1988 Item 208 in the catalogue of Orders, Medals and Decorations for auction at Sotheby's read:

The Unique and Important 'Cockleshell Heroes' DSM Group to Corporal W.E. 'Bill' Sparks, Royal Marines (8) comprising: Distinguished Service Medal, Geo. VI (Mne), 1939–45 Star, Atlantic Star, Africa Star, Italy Star, Burma Star, Defence Medal, War Medal.

An anonymous bidder paid £31,000 for them. Bill Sparks had saved his home and had enough for a small pension, which would keep him and his wife comfortable for the remainder of their lives. To this day, Bill's benefactor and owner of the Cockleshell Hero's medals remains unknown.

John Kirtley
Keeper of the Doors, House of Lords

As ex-Sergeant-Major John Kirtley strides purposefully along the plush stately corridors of the House of Lords, occasionally nodding a greeting to an ageing peer or venerable churchman, he is well aware that he is part of one of the world's most exclusive clubs – the Palace of Westminster. He is crisply dressed in a black-tailed suit, starched white shirt with matching bow tie. The glinting chain of office around his neck stands out in bright relief against his dark attire. Even his work within the House of Lords has that rare touch of vintage exclusivity. His official role – once held by titled men and princes – is Keeper of the Doors. He is one of a staff of twenty-five in the House of Lords.

In this rarefied atmosphere of political power and connivance, lesser men might be overawed. But ex-Marines do not readily succumb to the vanity of individuals. As John Kirtley says, 'By the very nature of our duties, we have a close association with all the peers. They never talk down to us and we are never subservient in any way.'

It would be naive for anybody to believe that these jobs are there for the asking. They are cherished positions, with well-paid bar and canteen privileges that enable one to rub shoulders with all the political bigwigs in the kingdom. All staff are issued with three made-to-measure 'uniforms' and receive an annual dry-cleaning allowance of £210. John Kirtley is frank: 'You never see the job advertised, you hear of it through the Old Boy network.'

There was a time when the Guards held most of the prestigious appointments in the Palace of Westminster, but in recent years it would appear that their Old Boy network has been in some disarray. The Marines have outmanoeuvred them and, for the time being at least, hold the balance of power. Though John Kirtley only works a 4-day week, the hours can be long, at times lasting until dawn, depending on the amount of legislation going through the House. As he points out 'Our facilities are excellent: there are "put-you-up" beds, hot showers and a fully equipped kitchen with a microwave oven.'

To refer to them as 'door keepers' can be misleading. They are part of the lubricating mechanism of Government and, like all civil servants, they may join a trade union if they wish. They ensure that the system ticks smoothly, and they represent an indispensable link in the bureaucratic chain. For not only are they part of the inner circle of security within the House of Lords, but they also sit in the Chamber as messengers and mark the Attendance Book of Peers. Their day begins at 2 p.m., except on Thursday when it is half an hour later, because of judgement being given in the Chamber.

John Kirtley is a Tynesider, and like many Geordies the brogue still lingers in his resonant, melodic voice. As a youngster he was keen on sport, so it is not surprising that he became an apprentice footballer with Everton, later playing for Sunderland as a professional. He remembers his pay, £7 a week – that was back in the 1960s. He enlisted in the Marines at twenty-three. As he says, "I joined a little later than most. My Marine pay at the time was less than I was making at football – about five pounds a week, as far as I can recall.'

What does he think of today's Marine? 'You have a much more intelligent guy in the Corps today. Before, there was a lot of "bull" – bullshit doesn't always baffle brains. Today he's a thinking man, now most of the "bull" has gone, he can clean his gear very quickly and get on with the job. I'm a great believer in standards – you must abide by them. I hear stories of shortcuts being taken – guys being given a green beret against the advice of instructors who don't think they meet the standards. I totally disagree with fudging, it represents a false picture and devalues the green beret.'

Do the NCOs run the Corps, as many of us are led to believe? He thinks carefully before replying and says, 'Young officers have to be guided. He will have been told by his Colonel to take notice of his NCOs and to "heed their warnings and heed their advice".' He continues, 'When the young officer starts to go over the top, then the seniors are always there to pull him into line and say, "Excuse me, Sir, may I suggest we do this?"'

Elaborating further, he says, 'The NCOs are a great guide to these young gentlemen. They are young and inexperienced and have to be led at times. That's where the seniors come in. The higher echelons of the officer corps will deny it – but on the other hand, they will do so with tongue in cheek. Sometimes I don't think they like or enjoy the "power" of the NCOs and would like to take it away from us. If they do, it will definitely reduce the efficiency of the troops on the ground, if they allow full power to the officers. The NCOs have a tremendous input into the Corps. We must also remember that the standard of the officer also reflects the standard of the NCO who has been guiding him.'

Surrounded as he is each day by centuries of pageantry and tradition, John Kirtley has developed a deep love for the Palace of Westminster. His is an enviable position, observing the powerful and mighty – amid the cut and thrust of politics – carving a place for themselves in order that they might hopefully become the legends of history.

Dave Morris
Police Sergeant, Falkland Islands Police

There is a timeless quality about life on a remote island that most of us, at some point or another, have yearned for, likely as not, in the depths of a grey, dismal British winter. As most will agree, this kind of island living is not for everyone. Many have tried it, only to find that the solitude is too overwhelming. Intellectually the process of adjustment will be a gradual process. The individual must become reconciled to the idea that he has escaped the monotonous conformity of one lifestyle – where everything was predictable, stylized, cut and dried – for the resplendent purity and isolation of another.

At first glance the stocky station Sergeant, in his well-pressed navy-blue uniform and chequered hat-band with its oversized cap badge, resembles any rural policeman seen on the streets of Britain's market towns throughout the year. There is a difference, however, in the small white-washed police station. With its red-coloured corrugated tin roof, weather-bleached, and neat white-painted wooden fence surrounding the trim lawn, it has a rustic charm reminiscent of Scotland's Western Isles or some quaint antipodean dwelling.

Dave Morris is a Liverpudlian and an ex-Marine. As a youngster running around the back streets of Merseyside, the thought that he would one day be a station Sergeant in the Falkland Islands Police never entered his head. At that time his world was no larger than a ride on the Mersey ferry.

It is more than likely that the Falkland Islands Police is one of the world's smallest constabularies: commanded by a Chief Constable with the rank of Superintendent, the force has sixteen Constables and two Sergeants. An Inspector has still to be appointed. Small it may be, but this is no back-woods law enforcement agency. Patrolling is done in Land Rovers, while a helicopter can be summoned if rapid transportation is needed to some distant part of the islands. There is a forensic laboratory, photographic unit, fingerprint bureau, and even breathalizer equipment for the Saturday night drunks. The immigration department is in the same building, as are six cells, which fulfil the needs of the islands' penal system. Three are detention cells, the others are for longer-term prisoners. Even police training presents few problems: Constables are trained locally by a Sergeant sent out from one of Britain's county forces, while specialist training is carried out in the United Kingdom.

Compared to many of his old colleagues in the Marines, who are disheartened by slow promotion and an eroding pay scale, Dave Morris has done well for himself and is to be envied. Look at his lifestyle: a way of life that he loves, reasonable hours of work, he sees his family every day, has a good salary and enjoys passage-paid leave to the United Kingdom every three years. What is more important, he has made Sergeant within five years of joining the force.

Sitting behind his desk in the neat office surrounded by all the paraphernalia of law and order, he looks the epitome of the British country bobby: a friendly countenance with just the right amount of authority and a voice that still betrays his Mersey roots. He talks about police work on the island.

'Most of the offences here are drink-related. There's a lot of drinking going on – not by everyone – by a minority of the population. Then there's quite a bit of criminal damage: theft of vehicle spares and that sort of thing. Land Rover parts are frequently stolen. There's not a great deal of crime in the camp [countryside]. Many of the minor things are taken care of by the farm managers. If there's an emergency we can get out there very quickly by helicopter.'

By the time he had served thirteen years in the Marines, Dave thought it was about time he got out. He was serving with the Falklands detachment at the time, and felt he had found the place where he would like to settle down, especially as he had fallen in love with a local girl, Alana, whom he was to marry. Of his early days in the Falklands he says, 'During the first couple of months here I didn't like it at all. Then after getting to know the people – I changed my mind.'

He married Alana on 6 February 1982, just a few weeks before the Argentinian invasion. As it turned out, when the Argentinians attacked Port Stanley, Dave Morris was escorting the diplomatic bag to Buenos Aires.

'Yes, I was on the wrong side of the fence. I was in my hotel room when I received a phone call from the Naval Attaché telling me to report to the Embassy right away. When I arrived they told me the invasion was imminent.' In Montevideo he rejoined his wife and returned to Britain.

Looking back on his time in the Marines he says, 'Initially I missed the Marines a lot, and I went through a period wondering if I had made the right decision. But you have to make the break some time. If you can fall on your feet when you do, it's a bonus.'

Can the young lad from the back streets of Liverpool who became a Marine and found himself living in the Falkland Islands see himself being the islands' top policeman one day? He smiles and is noncommittal, replying, 'I never even thought of being a policeman!'

David Brian Swayne – 'Spudge'
Landscape gardener and brickworker

When Marine Swayne no. PO40928D appeared before his Commanding Officer for the customary 'Why are you leaving the Corps?' chat, and was asked what he planned for the future, he replied in his quiet, matter-of-fact manner that he had not the faintest idea. Dave instinctively knew that it was time to get out of the Corps before it was too late. He had no intention of becoming the 20-year military man. Besides, he had done his bit for Queen and country. While still a teenager, this quiet, rangy Sussex lad – he was eighteen at the time – had been sent to war in the South Atlantic.

'I know my parents worried a lot when there was a rumour that the *Canberra* had been hit,' he says.

Dave survived the war with all his limbs intact. Like many war veterans, he is reticent at talking about the Falklands. He has to be comfortable and at ease with someone first.

'I was with 40 Commando and landed with "B" Company in the dark just before dawn. My feet were wet from go, as we had to wade ashore. That was a right downer, I can tell you.'

How Dave made it ashore with all the kit he had to carry, only he can tell, for not only did he have a 70-pound pack on his back and his personal weapon, but an 84mm anti-tank weapon with two shells, two 81mm mortar bombs and a 50-round belt of machine-gun ammunition.

'I stayed around San Carlos Water most of the time, as part of the rearguard defences, taking turns to go up to Windy Gap and Mount Kent to do OPs [Observation Positions]. One of the Corporals that trained me was killed out there. We came under air attack on several occasions – but we all survived.'

Like many youngsters before him, Dave Swayne joined the Marines when he was a little over sixteen. That was in 1980. He enlisted straight from school. Why did he join? Dave thinks it was for the adventure, and later to prove to himself that he had what it takes to wear the green beret. At Lympstone he joined Troop 267; there were seventy-two of them when training began. 'There were no more than fifteen of the original troop left when we finished our training,' he recalls.

Dave Swayne survived the rigours of training and Marine life in general because he has an inner spiritual strength that pulls him through. 'I'm not religious,' he explains, 'but I believe in being honest and never doing a man down. At the same time I know my worth in life. Family is very important to me.'

No doubt it was Dave's inner qualities that enabled him to survive his thirty weeks of training, in spite of Corporals who threw kit out of the window if it was not up to standard, or who, when out in the field, had you go to ground in gorse bushes as punishment for some misdemeanour or other. 'One minute you hate the Corporals – anybody would – but they were fair and honest. If they weren't strict and hard on you, you might as well be in the Army. After all, if you're going to be a Marine, you've got to have it, so you've got to take what they dish up. Yes, the training was tough,' he confesses, 'but it taught you to think for yourself.'

Of the officers he says, 'The young ones are all right, as long as they don't think they know it all. An officer who has made it through the ranks gets a lot more respect than someone who has started off in training as a Lieutenant. Yes, the NCOs certainly run the Corps. After all, they teach everyone. They have the knowledge and the experience.'

Like many Marines of his generation, Dave saw quite a bit of the world, something that today's Marine sorely misses, due to the cutbacks in overseas postings. He spent time in the West Indies, Belize, Gibraltar and various parts of the United States. Looking back he says, 'When I left the Marines I had a couple of hundred pounds in the bank and not the faintest idea what I was going to do: I never intended to stay in. I wanted to live my own life and learn a trade – you can't learn a trade in the Marines, can you? It's all about fighting. Besides, it's no good for married life, as far as I'm concerned. You're away so much. Husbands and wives begin to lead their own lives. There's a lot of messing about, which leads to marriage breakdowns.'

Looking back he knows that deep down there are things he will never forget. 'The Falklands, when the bombs fell on us. Doing the 30-miler in eight hours. My mum and dad coming to see me get my green beret.'

Dave Swayne is not one for joining the old comrades' association or wearing the Corps' tie, though he is proud of having once been a Marine. Once in a while, with a few close friends, he will look at souvenir photographs from his days in the Corps.

On 2 April 1985, Marine Swayne said farewell to the Corps and became a civilian. He had been a Marine for nearly five years. After leaving the Marines, Dave took a City and Guilds course, which enabled him to work in the building trade. His childhood sweetheart had waited for him over the years and on a bright summer's day in August 1989, surrounded by their parents and friends, they were married in the lovely Norman church of St Anne's in his home town of Lewes in East Sussex.

CONCLUSION, AND THE WAY AHEAD

As the twilight years of the twentieth century ebb away, the question of defence and military preparedness is causing growing concern within the Armed Forces. The Soviets are now less war-like. The philosophy of armed might is in decline. While the West struggles to interpret the shifting political sands throughout the Eastern Bloc, the British defence establishment is experiencing an unnerving time. There is a growing awareness within the British military community that the politicians are about to swing the proverbial fiscal axe. It is all a question of political expediency: the environment is a far better vote-winner than defence. Across the Atlantic there is naught but cold comfort from the Americans. According to recent reports (1989), they have every intention of cutting their defence budget by 20 per cent over the next five years. At home, with an anticipated zero-growth defence budget, currently standing at £22.2 billion (1990–1), Britain's service chiefs are edgy. Though final agreement has not yet been reached, among the options being considered are:

- a 25 per cent cut in the defence budget by the end of the decade
- a 40 per cent cut in equipment budgeting
- a 50 per cent reduction in the defence industry employment
- the disbanding and merging of many regiments
- a review of key projects, such as the European fighter aircraft and the new army tank.

So where does this leave the Royal Marines, and what will be their future role? Regardless of the Government's loyalties towards the Corps, will the Royal Marines, as we know them, exist in the year 2000?

In this jingoistic Thatcher era of sovereignty preservation, for the time being at least, the future of the Marines appears assured. After all, they were the vanguard of the Falklands campaign, which helped to secure a political victory for Thatcher's Government. However, politicians have short memories. Unlike Generals, they are quick to forget the conflicts they helped to inspire. Yesterday's foes, we are told, are now people with whom we can do business. Cold-War politics have been cast aside. Europe has been convulsed by revolution.

Nations have been liberated. The traditional 'Reds under the bed' syndrome is crumbling fast.

There is little doubt that among the world's military communities the Royal Marines are perceived as a crack force of professional individuals, who have no rivals. They are trained with the same intensity, and come from the same caste, as the ancient *samurai*. As we have witnessed, in combat they are the last of the true warriors. For in this push-button age of military conflict, they remain among the few who meet the enemy eyeball to eyeball. Such men represent a disappearing breed.

British alchemy for Marine-making is right. Through years of fine-tuning the Corps has arrived at a formula for training the world's finest infantry commando. He is neither a zealot, robotic, puritan-minded nor overtly gung-ho. It may seem trite to proclaim that the Marine commando is intelligent, highly motivated, and with an inbred spirit of good old-fashioned Anglo-Saxon doggedness, yet he is just that. The Corps, in its wisdom, is tolerant and broad-minded. It has, much to its credit, relinquished many of the old regimental rites and rubrics, leaving room for the individual and the occasional nonchalant rogue. By all accounts the Corps does not have a 'black problem', like other units of the British Army. In many ways it is the reverse: anxious as they are to show their impartiality, the Marines fail to attract blacks or the ethnic minorities into the ranks of the officer corps in sufficient numbers. It concerns them, for in this age of the multi-cultural society, naturally they are sensitive to being labelled something they are not – racially biased. Along with the Special Air Service (SAS), there is little doubt that the Corps is the only place remaining in the British military system for the 'one-off'. Thankfully, the Marines recognize that campaigns are won by men such as the Wingates and the Montgomerys.

For all this, perhaps the real test of the Marines' ability to survive is yet to come. They are in something of a dilemma, and are increasingly facing fundamental problems. They must adapt quickly – which they are very capable of doing – to the politics and needs of a rapidly changing world.

As any Marine, from Bootneck to General, will tell you, one of their major roles has been as guardian of NATO's northern flank. The reinforcement of Norway, alongside the Dutch Marine Corps, 'is very much a principal justification for their existence and their mode of living', one military observer remarked. Year after year they have sharpened their fighting skills in the frozen wastes and fiords of Norway. As Arctic warriors there are none better. A Marine commando has learnt how to survive and fight in hostile terrain. But as a NATO confrontation with the Soviet Union and what was referred to as the Warsaw Pact countries recedes further and further into a historical existence, the Marines' role in that part of the world is becoming increasingly obsolete. As one commentator remarked, 'The Marines have hung their hats almost solely on their Norwegian role, together with certain out-of-area roles, like the Falklands. They could find themselves something of a one-legged animal!' The simple truth is that the northern flank no longer exists.

The Soviet Union is in the first stages of revolution, and its leaders are embroiled in saving what they can of the Motherland. New dilemmas are emerging which need our vigilance – Islamic fundamentalism and state terrorism are but two. New shapes are emerging in Europe; the old outlines are disappearing. Somewhere among the emerging forms are the leaders of future uprisings. Who knows, perhaps a new 'Tsar' will rise from the ashes?

It is not in the nature of the Marines to become an anachronism, a malady that is endemic to the British regimental system. They are too proud and spirited for that. Yet they must find a new role for themselves as the complexion of NATO undergoes osmosis from military deterrent to political broker. In addition, as an amphibious force the Marines are well aware that the days of large-scale beach landings are a thing of the past. Given the run-down state of the country's mercantile fleet, most military strategists will agree that even a Falklands-type operation could no longer be considered. As the threat of large-scale conventional war fades, it will be in the area of low intensity, Third World and Middle East confrontation that the Corps' skills will be most needed.

A source with an excellent knowledge of military affairs explained. 'During the next twenty years we will need intervention forces – like the Marines and the paras – in places we have tended to forget about. The Horn of Africa, Oman, Cyprus, Iran – look at India bullying Sri Lanka at the moment! We cannot pretend that the Middle East is non-existent. And let us not forget Hong Kong.' Elaborating further, he went on to say that there was a real need for a rapid intervention force, made up of all the Western European nations, which could deal with skirmishes in such contentious areas of the world.

Should the Marines become involved in the Gulf Crisis in any significant numbers, like the rest of the British Forces there, they would be untrained and ill-equipped for desert warfare. As far as can be ascertained, there are no fluent Arabic speaking senior officers in the Marines; a serious disadvantage for any westerner operating in the Gulf. Equipment and clothing have to be modified, and all officers and NCOs given a crash course in colloquial Arabic before the Marines can venture into the area with any effectiveness. The desert has little respect for the mechanical and technical age, so it would not be at all bizarre for a specialist Troop to be formed which was trained to handle and ride camels. Living like the Bedouin, a Marine Camel Troop would be invaluable in reconnaissance and intelligence gathering.

In the light of the civil war in Romania, surely there is a case for inviting the Soviet Union to contribute specialist forces to the project? Consider how much sooner the conflict could have ended, how many more lives could have been saved, if such a pan-European military force had been available. Provided that it has the right kind of ships, specially constructed to meet its needs – in effect, modern-day commando carriers – the strength of an amphibious force, such as the Royal Marines, is that it can remain offshore for a relatively indefinite time, waiting until it is required for a specific operation. Surely there is a case for combining the expertise of the Royal Marines and the Parachute Regiment to form a rapid deployment strike force?

There is another area where the Marines could be most effective. As the problem of dealing with drug-smugglers becomes more acute and the resources of the police, customs and drug-enforcement agencies are extended, undoubtedly there is a role here for the Corps. Within the Royal Marines there is a pool of expertise unrivalled anywhere in the United Kingdom – men who are experts with small boats, and who have all the chicanery to outwit the drug-runners. Such units have been highly successful in Hong Kong, and surely there is no reason why another specialist Raiding Squadron should not be formed to combat the drug menace to Britain's shores?

Although it has little in common with the Royal Marines, the United States Marine Corps casts an envious eye on the way the 'Royals' do things. One USMC Colonel had this to say about the Corps.

'The Royal Marines train to specific functions, more so than we do. What General Gray [USMC] likes about the Corps [RM] is that they are all warriors, and that's where he would like to get back to also.' The Colonel elaborated, 'He also wants to instil in the USMC the commando-type spirit and skills – the toughness, and the mountain and Arctic warfare abilities.'

There are things that worry the US Marines about their 'British brethren-in-arms', as they like to think of the Royal Marines. From an American point of view, Marines should have their own ships and air cover. Royal Marines have neither. For their amphibious capability they rely solely on the Royal Navy, as they do for any form of troop-carrying helicopter. Ideally the Americans would like to see the Corps become a self-contained force like themselves. As they see it, the Royal Marines are vulnerable from the air. Calling on the Navy or the Air Force reduces efficiency, as far as the Americans are concerned. Most experts, including some of the Corps' top brass, agree that the Marines' helicopter capability is meagre. One source, a keen observer of Britain's military, said, 'Helicopters are everybody's Cinderella. If there's a bit of money left over in the budget, then they'll buy some.' He went on, 'Either they get into the comprehensive all-arms business – like the US Marines – or they don't. I suspect they realize that it would be outside their resources to do that.'

These days a profound melancholy pervades the ranks of the Royal Marines, for they just cannot keep their men in the Corps. It is not simply a question of Marine Bloggs throwing his hand in because something or other about the Corps has made him disgruntled. It is more serious and more complex than that. Resignations are rampant throughout the Corps, from the 4-year Marine to the once career-minded Colonel. In the past year (1989/90) there was an unconfirmed figure of 2,700 leaving the Corps. Some have reached the end of their 20-year stint. However, it would appear that the greater part are leaving to begin new careers. Most Marines are merely changing uniforms – their expertise is eagerly sought by police forces, the prison service, fire departments and private security firms. Officers, tired of waiting to fill dead men's shoes and remorselessly chasing promotion by way of the cocktail and dinner circuit, are searching for juicy corporate appointments to meet the ever-rising cost of mortgages and public school fees. Where do these men end up?

A former Lieutenant-Colonel with over twenty-seven years' service in the Corps, holder of the Military Cross, Falklands veteran and campaigner in other 'bush war' confrontations, deliberated for eighteen months before, as he put it, he 'saw the red light'. Speaking about his decision to leave the Corps, he says, 'I summed up my chances quite coldly and analytically and decided that by the age of fifty-one I would not make a two-star General. I knew that I could get to full Colonel by the time I was due for retirement. So I thought, if I am going to go, I will go now at forty-five, get a good job in civilian life that will take me to sixty and, hopefully, beyond. I have seen far too many good men in the Corps over the years who have almost made it, but they have been given the golden handshake at fifty-one.'

As the crisp morning sunlight filters through the bay window of his newly purchased country home, he explains further, 'I weighed up what was happening to the British Armed Forces in this age of *glasnost* and *perestroika*, and the impact that this was going to have – most certainly a defence review, reduction in resources, reduction in world profile for the British Forces, which have been reducing since the last war but will probably take a bit of a nose-dive over the next ten years. Balancing that with my own promotion prospects, I decided that the time had come to go. I went to a firm in London which specializes in placing people, and paid them five thousand pounds. They taught me how to write a c.v. and sell myself to a large corporation. As you can see, it worked reasonably well. I am now running a Family Health Services Authority. I manage a budget of about eighty-five million pounds and have a staff of seventy. During the past twelve months, five Colonels have prematurely left the Corps. There are others who I know have looked at what I have done, and are weighing up what their future chances are in the Corps – wondering whether to stay in or go outside. I suppose you could say that I was one of the first rats to leave the sinking ship. On the other hand, the Corps has always taken pride in teaching its officers to think for themselves.'

In Hong Kong a former Captain was made an offer he could not refuse by an international financial institution. He loved the Corps, agonized over his decision, but saw little future with the Marines and departed. Another, a young Lieutenant, resigned his commission and went into the travel business. Some seek Army careers, where promotion is more attractive. Others, sensing they are rank-frozen, resign in the hope that something will turn up in the world outside the Corps.

The Marines put a brave face on it all. The

official line is that they are up to strength and have a waiting list to enter the Corps. Meanwhile, they continue to lose highly experienced men and have no foreseeable remedy. One solution would be to recruit women directly into the Corps, replacing the present system of women serving with the Marines by way of the WRNS. However, an observer of the Royal Marines remarked, 'They are an amazing reactionary organization. Old-fashioned – what we've got is good – and resistant to change.'

A young prince from Britain's Royal family joining the Marines was a problem of a different kind. If there is one single thing that the Royal Marines would like erased from their history books, it is the Edward saga. At first, no doubt, the Corps believed it had made a fine catch when the Monarch's youngest son decided to join them. It could undoubtedly have strengthened their arm in the corridors of power. In no time at all, however, the affair became a fiasco. How such a crack force could display such naivety in dealing with the press and the prince's security is difficult to comprehend. The press milked it for all it was worth. Now the jokes are fewer, the cartoons less frequent. Unofficially the Corps recognizes that serious errors of judgement were made. It is learning to live with the episode and, while it does not care to laugh at the matter, at least it is now able to smile ambivalently about the prince who attempted to be one of them. Senior officers murmur quiet platitudes when questioned about his highly publicized departure, replying, 'He did well in training ... would have made a good officer...It was His Royal Highness's decision...'

One Marine observer made this laconic remark, 'The Marines should not have encouraged him to try. There was a public failure on Edward's part and on the Marines' part to get it right. It's very germane, in a way. The Edward saga was a mirror into the soul of the Corps!'

There is a fraternalism both within and outside the Corps that is near masonic. Marines stick together; their corporate identity is lifelong. Jobs are whispered down the grapevine; they join each other's clubs and congregate to support the Corps whenever the need arises. Around the hallowed halls of the Palace of Westminster more than a score of ex-Marines serve the legislative arm of the nation. Though small in number, they still have a great deal of influence in high places.

Outsiders are rarely privy to debates on the future of the Corps. Any attempt to query the system is met with smooth polemic and confident PR phrases, proclaiming, 'All is well, long live the Marines...' Deep down, though, Marines are aware that their future is in question. There is a growing concern from within and outside the Corps that the Royal Marines, in their present form, may not survive beyond the first decade of the twenty-first century. As one officer said, 'I wonder if we'll be around fifteen years from now.' Survival, on the other hand, is their stock-in-trade. They are taught to be cunning, tenacious to the extreme, and to fight with artful professionalism. They have been showing the world for over 300 years that they are able to out-wit, out-manoeuvre, out-scheme, out-connive and out-shoot anyone who crosses their path. They thrive on adversity and relish a fight. The greater the odds, the better they like it. Their tribalism is so tight that they will never surrender. After all, they will tell you, 'What matters most is the Corps. Let's go for it, lads!'

HISTORICAL
SECTION

THE MILITARY BACKGROUND

1664

By decree of Charles II, the Duke of York and Albany's Maritime Regiment of Foot was formed on 28 October 1664, from which the Royal Marines was founded. The regiment became known as the Lord High Admiral's Regiment, or the Admiral's Regiment.

1690

Two Marine regiments were formed – the 1st and 2nd Marine Regiments. They were disbanded in 1699.

1704

1,800 British and Dutch Marines attacked Gibraltar, which surrendered to the British on 24 July 1704.

1755

The Marine Mutiny Act (1755) brought about the formation of independent Marine companies. Marines were stationed at Portsmouth, Plymouth and Chatham. Historians regard this as the beginning of the present-day Marine Corps.

1761

Battle of Belle-Île, 7 June 1761: commanded by Lieutenant-Colonel John McKenzie, two battalions of Marines took part in the first seaborne landing during the siege of Belle-Île, near Quiberon Bay in Brittany.

1775

The Battle of Bunker Hill, 17 June 1775: a Marine force, commanded by Major John Pitcairn, overcame an American rebel force that was dominating high ground to the north of Boston, where a British garrison was located. During the engagement to retake the hill it is recorded that twenty-nine Marines were killed and eighty-seven wounded.

1788

Marines were present at the raising of the Union Jack, commemorating the founding of Sydney, Australia. According to early records, twenty-one officers and 192 Marines volunteered for a three-year period of service, together with some forty wives, in the penal colony of Botany Bay, New South Wales.

The Marines landing at Gibraltar, 21 July, 1704, an illustration which originally appeared in Cannon's *Records of the 4th Regiment*

'The Death of Major John Pitcairn at Bunker Hill' by J. Trumbwell

'The Founding of Australia' (Sydney Cove, 26 January 1788, with a guard of Royal Marines from HMS *Supply*)

1793

The French Revolutionary Wars, 1793–1802: Marines were involved in campaigns in Corsica, South Africa, India, Egypt, Palestine and the East Indies, as well as various naval engagements including Camperdown, the Nile and Cape St Vincent.

1802

On the recommendation of Admiral Lord St Vincent, George III commanded that the Royal prefix should be granted to the Marines on 29 April 1802.

1805

The Battle of Trafalgar, 21 October 1805: ninety-two officers and 2,600 Marines took part in the Battle of Trafalgar. Marine casualites were: four officers and 113 Marines killed, and thirteen officers and 212 Marines wounded. Lord Nelson was held by Sergeant Secker of the Royal Marines as he lay mortally wounded on the deck of HMS *Victory*. Writing to his sister, a survivor of the battle, Private James Bagley, said, 'it was very sharp for us, I can assure you.'

1855

Marines served at the Siege of Sebastopol. Bombardier T. Wilkinson, Royal Marine Artillery (RMA), was awarded the Victoria Cross (see Victoria Crosses of the Royal Marines).

1899

The Boer War, 1899–1902: Marines with mobile guns were in action at Graspan. Marines and seamen were used as assault infantry.

1900

The Boxer Uprising, 1900–1: Royal Marines, along with the US Marines, were involved in the relief of Peking.

1903

The Royal Marine Band Service was formed according to an order in council dated 20 May 1903. Band Boys were paid eightpence per day, and a Chief Bandmaster (Warrant Officer) five shillings and sixpence halfpenny a day. Musicians were paid a further twopence a day for careful maintenance of their instruments.

Royal Marine Light Infantrymen at Flathouse Quay, Portsmouth, 1896, with the training hulks HMS *Duke of Wellington* and HMS *Marlborough* at left, HMS *Asia* at right

12th Battalion, Royal Marines embarking for Shanghai on the transport ship *Minnesota* at south railway jetty, Portsmouth harbour, 25 January 1927

1914

The First World War, 1914–18: Marines served on ships which were in action at Jutland, the Falkland Islands and Dogger Bank. On land, Marines were in action within five days of the German advance into France and Belgium. 1st and 2nd Royal Marine Light Infantry (RMLI) battalions returned from Gallipoli to France and were reorganized, some into machine-gun companies. In 1918 these two battalions were combined to form the 1st RMLI.

In 1915, a Howitzer Brigade (Bde) was formed, comprising ten specially constructed 15-inch howitzers, manned by crews of five officers and eighty-three other ranks.

1915

The Gallipoli Landings, 28 April 1915: the Royal Marine Brigade's casualties amounted to twenty-one officers and 217 other ranks killed, twenty-nine officers and 764 other ranks wounded. 122 others were reported missing.

For his outstanding courage and devotion to duty, Lance Corporal Walter Richard Parker of the Royal Marines Light Infantry was awarded the Victoria Cross, together with the 1914–15 Star, British War and Victory Medal.

1918

The Zeebrugge Raid, 23 April 1918: the German naval base at Zeebrugge was attacked by the 4th Battalion Royal Marines, led by its commander, Lieutenant-Colonel B.N. Elliot, DSO, on St George's Day 1918. Casualties included Lt-Col Elliot, his second-in-command, Major Cordner, nine other officers and 109 NCOs and Marines. 233 of all ranks were wounded, and nineteen taken prisoner. The Marines were awarded two Victoria Crosses.

1922

During the following seventeen years Royal Marines served in Ireland (1922), Constantinople and Shanghai, as well as on board ships of the Royal Navy.

1939–45

The Second World War: throughout the war Royal Marines, and the newly formed Royal Marine Commandos, were involved in worldwide operations from Western Europe to the South Pacific.

In Western Europe, Marines were in action in Norway, Holland and France, and Marines of the 1st Commando Brigade crossed the Rhine with the Allied advance into Germany. In Italy, RM Commandos (40 and 43) fought their way through the flooded Po Valley, where the Germans surrendered on 3 May 1945. 16,000 Royal Marines were involved in the Normandy Landings on 6 June 1944. Most of the landing craft were manned by Royal Marines and all capital ships carried a Royal Marine Detachment. Five Royal Marine Commandos (41, 45, 46, 47 and 48) landed during the assault phase, grouped with three Army Commandos into two Special Service Brigades. In addition, the Corps provided a number of specialist units, including an Armoured Support Group, Beach Clearance and Control Parties, as well as Engineers. During the Normandy campaign, Royal Marines received seventy gallantry awards, including five DSOs', thirteen DSCs and thirteen MMs. On 1 November 1944 Marines participated in the assault on Walcheren in Holland.

In the Mediterranean, Marines were in action in Malta, Crete, Tobruk, Sicily, Italy, Albania and Yugoslavia.

In South-East Asia and the Pacific, Marines were involved in operations in Malaya, in the defence of Singapore, Burma, raids on the Arakan coast, and landings on Cheduba Island, Myebon and Kangaw. Throughout the war, the Royal Marines served on board Royal Navy ships in a number of roles.

1948

The Royal Marines, along with other British troops, secured the withdrawal from Palestine.

1950

Malaya: Royal Marines involved in anti-terrorist operations. Korea: 41 (Independent) Commando was in a fighting retreat on the Chosin Plateau, alongside the 1st United States Marine Division. The Commando was awarded a United States Presidential citation. After returning to Korea as a raiding force, the Commando was disbanded in 1952.

Royal Marines in Catania, Sicily, August 1943

42 Commando river patrol, Borneo, 1966

1953
Canal Zone, Egypt: 40 Commando was on internal security duties.

1955
Anti-terrorist operations by 40 and 45 Commando in Cyprus.

1956
The Suez Crisis: as part of the Anglo-French force, the Commando Brigade (40, 42 and 45 Cdo), landed to take Port Said.

1960
Between 1960 and 1967 Marines of 45 Commando were involved in operations in Aden and Radfan.

1962
Four years of anti-terrorist operations in North Borneo and West Malaysia by 40 and 42 Commando.

1964
Marine Commandos in East Africa.

1969
Northern Ireland: first of the emergency tours undertaken by the Royal Marine Commandos, which continue to the present day (1991) for a period of four to five months.

1970
Royal Marine Commandos of 45 Commando commenced Arctic training. In Bangladesh, Marines came to the aid of flood victims.

1972
Royal Marines Logistics Regiment was formed. In June in Northern Ireland 'Operation Motorman' took place.

1974
Marines of 40 and 41 Commando went to Cyprus during the period of the invasion by the Turkish military.

1976
42 Commando commenced duties in Hong Kong. Monitoring teams went to Southern Rhodesia. Royal Marine detachments in frigates off Iceland, in Cod War.

1980

In May, 41 Commando was disbanded.

1982

Royal Marines have provided a small garrison on the Falkland Islands since the nineteenth century. The recapture of the Falkland Islands, 14 June 1982: a total of 3,520 Marines took part in one of the most ambitious amphibious landings in history. Conveyed 8,000 miles from their United Kingdom base, the Royal Marines were involved in every aspect of the retaking of the islands. The main landing was planned and put into operation by Marines of 3 Commando Brigade (40, 42 and 45 Commando). Two officers and twenty-five men were killed during the campaign and sixty-seven were wounded. The following honours and awards were made to the Royal Marines: one KCB, one CB, two DSOs, six OBES, three MBES, two DSCS, five MCS, two DFCS, ten MMS, one DCM, three DSMS, one DFM, and one QGM.

K Company, 42 Commando on Mount Kent, East Falkland before the attack on Mount Harriet, 11 June 1982

THE MARENS

The Women's Royal Naval Service has had a connection with the Royal Marines since its earliest days. On 29 November 1917 *The Times* carried an advertisement announcing the Admiralty's decision to establish the service to undertake various duties on shore, in order to release male personnel for other work. They became known as the 'Wrens' and began to take posts as clerks, mess waiters and cooks, later training in wireless telegraphy. Some also worked as boat crews in harbour, a duty they were able to perform on a larger scale in the Second World War.

In common with naval establishments, each Royal Marines barracks received its draft of Wrens, but soon their name turned to 'Marens', when detachments were appointed to the Corps. Miss Lettice Clarke was among the first group of Marens to arrive at Eastney in 1917. She was fortunate to have her uniform, as most members of the service did not receive theirs until January 1918. By the end of the war 7,000 women had volunteered for service in the WRNS, although in 1919 the service was disbanded until 21 February 1939.

During the Second World War, Marens were again employed but with an even wider range of duties. They worked as mechanics, armourers, boat crews, cypher clerks, drivers, packers, storekeepers and writers, and were also involved in early radar, meteorology and radio communications. They were also responsible for repairing torpedo mechanisms, one of their many technical duties.

When serving with Royal Marines units, the tally band on the hat was replaced by a red patch set behind the Globe and Laurel badge, which, according to Mrs Amy Blake who served as a Maren at this time, 'made the girls feel extra special'.

Since the Second World War Marens have continued to work with Royal Marines units in many different ways, and have served with them in such diverse places as Gibraltar, Northern Ireland, Norway and Hong Kong.

General L.S.T. Halliday vc inspects cadets of the Royal Marines Girls Ambulance Corps at Plymouth in 1929 (the Corps was similar to the boys' Royal Marines Cadet units, but girls learnt first aid rather than military skills)

G. R.

Royal Marines.

WANTED,

A few young Men and Lads to complete the above distinguished Corps.

Young Men defirous of enroling themfelves will receive the

HIGHEST BOUNTIES AND EVERY ENCOURAGEMENT.

The *Advantages* of ferving in this *old eftablifhed Corps* are generally known : while on Shore they are ftationed in comfortable Barracks, on board Ship they have the *fame Allowances* as the *Navy ;* befides their Pay they receive one pound of the beft Beef, one ditto of Bread, Flour, Butter, Cheefe, Tea, Sugar, &c. and a pint of the beft Wine, or half a pint of the *ftrongeft Brandy* or *Rum.* They likewife fhare in *Prize Money* with the *Navy,* by which *thoufands.* have acquired *confiderable Fortunes,* and are enabled to return to their Friends in *Comfort* and *Independence.*

In Addition to the above Advantages, when embarked they can allot half of their Pay to their Wives or Relations, which will be paid them by the Collectors at their Places of Refidence.

Young Men or Lads, wifhing to enter into the ROYAL MARINES, will meet with the moft kind and honourable Treatment, by applying at the

ROYAL MARINE RENDEZVOUS,

Square & Compasses, Dale-street, Liverpool;

N. B. Such Recruits as can write and behave well, will be fure of Promotion.

A School Mafter is appointed to inftruct thofe who wifh to poffefs the great Advantages of Learning.

BRINGERS OF GOOD RECRUITS WILL RECEIVE THREE GUINEAS.

GOD SAVE THE KING.

T. KAYE, Printer to his Royal Highnefs the DUKE of GLOUCESTER and EDINBURGH.

PAY AND CHARGES

Royal Marines Basic Pay*

monthly pay

Junior from the age of 16$^{1}/_{2}$ £309
Junior from the age of 17......................................£375
Junior doing Marine 2nd Class duties £496
Marine 2nd Class £496–563
Marine 1st Class £641–806
Corporal £872–1,013
Sergeant...£1,072–1,124
Colour Sergeant £1,167–1,238
WO II..£1,312–1,335
WO I..£1,391–1,414

*A pay rise of 8 per cent was awarded in 1990.

Charges
Food: a continuous daily charge is levied in shore establishments at home and abroad. Men are not charged when serving afloat. The charge is £80.60 (31-day month) for single personnel and £40.30 for married unaccompanied.

Accommodation: there is a charge of between £13.02 and £69.75 a month, according to rank, for single accommodation. Accommodation charges may now be reduced slightly to compensate for the Community Charge.

Married quarters: the standard charges for furnished quarters in England and Wales range between £75.64 and £140.12 a month for RM other ranks.

Royal Marines Officers' Basic Pay*

annual pay

2nd Lieutenant RM on appointment £8,428
Graduate, on entry as Sub-Lieutenant RN or
    2nd Lieutenant RM £9,662
Lieutenant......................................£12,713–18,812
Captain...£20,404–24,433
Major £28,050–30,999
Lieutenant-Colonel..........................£32,346–34,047
Colonel £38,748

*A pay rise of 8 per cent was awarded in 1990.

Flying Pay

additional annual pay

Pilot and Observer during flying training, until
    award of Wings £365
Lieutenant-Colonel RM £2,978
Colonel RM..£1,896

Charges
Food: a charge which averages £79.08 a month is levied on single officers accommodated in shore establishments at home and abroad. There is no charge when serving afloat.

Accommodation: officers 'living in' pay a monthly charge for standard accommodation ashore. This varies between £45.00 and £117.18.

Married quarters: charges are payable for living in the service's married quarters, at varying rates.

Fairey III F and two Ripons of 806 Squadron, HMS *Glorious* flying over Malta in 1931. The pilots were the Royal Marine Lieutenants W.S. North (806), J.L. Moulton (73) and N.R.M. Skene (64)

ROYAL MARINES ORGANIZATION

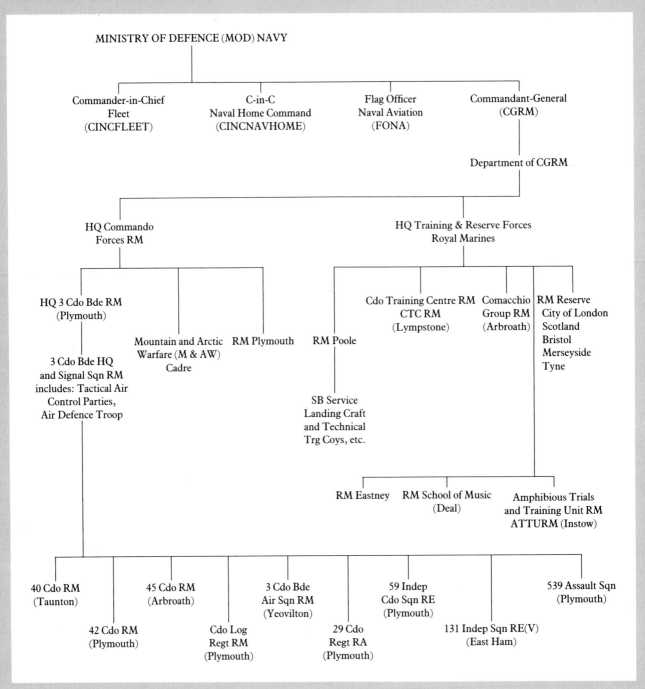

MINISTRY OF DEFENCE (MOD) NAVY

Commander-in-Chief Fleet (CINCFLEET)

C-in-C Naval Home Command (CINCNAVHOME)

Flag Officer Naval Aviation (FONA)

Commandant-General (CGRM)

Department of CGRM

HQ Commando Forces RM

HQ Training & Reserve Forces Royal Marines

HQ 3 Cdo Bde RM (Plymouth)

3 Cdo Bde HQ and Signal Sqn RM includes: Tactical Air Control Parties, Air Defence Troop

Mountain and Arctic Warfare (M & AW) Cadre

RM Plymouth

RM Poole

Cdo Training Centre RM CTC RM (Lympstone)

Comacchio Group RM (Arbroath)

RM Reserve City of London Scotland Bristol Merseyside Tyne

SB Service Landing Craft and Technical Trg Coys, etc.

RM Eastney

RM School of Music (Deal)

Amphibious Trials and Training Unit RM ATTURM (Instow)

40 Cdo RM (Taunton)

42 Cdo RM (Plymouth)

45 Cdo RM (Arbroath)

Cdo Log Regt RM (Plymouth)

3 Cdo Bde Air Sqn RM (Yeovilton)

29 Cdo Regt RA (Plymouth)

59 Indep Cdo Sqn RE (Plymouth)

131 Indep Sqn RE(V) (East Ham)

539 Assault Sqn (Plymouth)

Notes

1 All field force units are under the operational command of HQ 3 Cdo Bde when this is in UK. When 3 Cdo Bde is abroad MGRM Cdo Forces assumes operational command of field force units remaining in UK.

2 Operational control of the following may be given to HQ 3 Cdo Bde: W Coy RNLMC (Dutch); 1 ACG RNLMC; SBS; Naval Air Sqns.

3 Drafting and Records Office RM is co-located with HMS *Centurion*.

172

ROYAL MARINES SCHOOL OF MUSIC'S ORGANIZATION

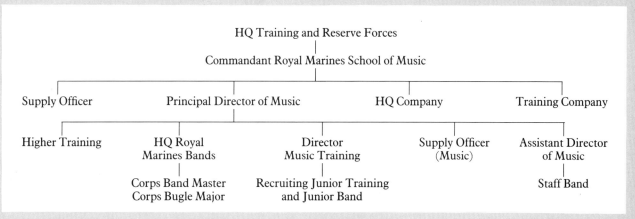

HQ Training and Reserve Forces
|
Commandant Royal Marines School of Music

Supply Officer	Principal Director of Music	HQ Company	Training Company

Higher Training	HQ Royal Marines Bands	Director Music Training	Supply Officer (Music)	Assistant Director of Music
	Corps Band Master Corps Bugle Major	Recruiting Junior Training and Junior Band		Staff Band

Staff and other bands

Most of these are responsible to the senior officer concerned, but their work is co-ordinated by the Department of CGRM and the Principal Director of Music. In 1985 there were four staff bands each of sixty-six musicians provided for C-in-C Fleet, C-in-C Naval Home Command, HMRM Commandos and the RM School of Music. Standard bands of around forty-two were appointed to Flag Officer Plymouth, to Flag Officer Scotland and Northern Ireland and to *Britannia* RN College.

RM Musicians provide orchestras and dance bands, as well as military bands, for both service occasions and public relations' activities.

REGIMENTAL MUSIC

Inspection Music

The 'Globe and Laurel', an arrangement of the tune 'Early One Morning', was the regimental slow march until 1964 and is often played during inspection on parade.

The Corps has three official marches which are played on ceremonial occasions:

The Commando March

The origins of the commando march 'Sarie Marais' are South African; it was the trekking song of the Afrikaner Boer Commandos. In 1937 Captain Vivian Dunn made a special arrangement of the old Boer song, and it was adopted by the Royal Marine Commandos in 1952. It is rarely omitted from any musical programme on Marine ceremonial occasions. The translation from the Afrikaans is as follows:

> Oh, take me back to the old Transvaal
> That's where I long to be,
> I left my little Sarie where the mallies grow
> Just by the green thorn tree
> And I'll be there to meet her

> Where I loved her so,
> Down by the green thorn tree.

'A Life on the Ocean Wave'

An arrangement of this song, with part of another song, 'The Sea', was first adopted as the regimental quick march of the Corps in 1882. The words are:

> A life on the ocean wave,
> A home on the rolling deep,
> Where the scatter'd waters rave
> And the winds their revels keep,
> Like an eagle cag'd I pine
> On this dull unchanging shore;
> O give me the flashing brine,
> The spray and the tempest's roar.

The Preobrajensky March

Lord Mountbatten presented this music to the Corps on the occasion of its tercentenary, as the regimental slow march. His uncle was one of the last Colonels of the Preobrajensky Guards, the senior regiment of the Imperial Russian Foot Guards.

UNIFORMS OF THE ROYAL MARINES

It is the distinctive white helmet, adorned with a brass ball and helmetplate on top, which, more than anything else, immediately distinguishes the Royal Marines from other military units in the British Armed Forces. The helmet has been part of Marine ceremonial dress since the early part of the twentieth century. The Royal Marines' ceremonial dress uniform is made of a navy-blue worsted material. The trousers have a thin scarlet stripe down the outside. Officers' dress is similar to regular Army dress, only in a light-weight blue material. Trousers have a quarter-inch scarlet strip down the outside seam. Senior officers have a broader stripe down the trouser seam. Field officers, adjutants and ADCs wear close-fitting trousers, with wellington boots and spurs for ceremonial occasions. All ranks wear the letters 'RM' in gilt on their shoulder straps. Collar badges are worn and are similar to the cap badge – a globe and laurel. Buttons are embossed with the foul anchor and crown, surrounded by the words 'Royal Marines', all within a laurel wreath.

As for the lovat uniform, first worn in April 1964, the dress is olive-green in colour and is made of a barathea-type material. Badges are identical to those of the blue uniform, only made of bronze.

Lanyards

Officers and WO1s wear a navy-blue silk lanyard on their left shoulder. Unit lanyards are worn by all commando ranks in lovat dress. They are displayed on the right shoulder with identifying colours: Headquarters Commando Forces, maroon; Commando Logistics Regiment, blue; Headquarters 3 Commando Brigade, dark green; 40 Commando, light blue; 42 Commando, white; 45 Commando, scarlet; Comacchio Group, gold and scarlet.

The Corps Badge

This comprises a lion and crown above a larger crown, sitting above a globe surrounded by a laurel wreath. Officers' and Warrant Officers' badges have been in two parts since the amalgamation of the RMLI and the RMA in 1923. There are two types of Corps badges, bronze and black. It was George IV, in 1827, who granted the globe to the Corps. It is traditionally accepted that the laurels were granted to the Marines for their part in the capture of Belle-Île in 1827.

Rank and Specialist Badges

Rank badges for the Royal Marines follow the same style as those for the British Army. Colonels and more senior officers wear Army rank badges; stars, crowns and gorget patches, with RM badges, buttons and blue lanyards.

Colour Sergeants wearing 'Blues' have their rank badge made in gold wire and consisting of three chevrons; on top is an embroidered globe over crossed Union Jacks, with a laurel wreath and crown above. All ranks wear the Royal Marines Commando flash on the upper part of the arms of woollen pullovers. The Band Service wears a similar shoulder flash with the designation 'Royal Marines Band Service'. Special qualification badges are a woven symbol worn on the sleeve, their position varying according to the qualification. First-class above-rank chevrons, second- and third-class are worn on the left cuff.

The King's Badge

The title King's Squad is given to the squad that is undergoing its final week of training. In 1918 King George V gave the senior recruit squad this title and at the same time commanded that the best all-round recruit be given an award – the King's Badge. Those receiving the award are always referred to in the Corps as King's Badgemen. Throughout their service, King's Badgemen wear the King's Badge on the upper part of their left sleeve.

The Prince's Badge

As with the King's Badge, if there is a candidate of sufficiently high standard, the best all-round musician or bugler completing training will be awarded the Prince's Badge. The award was instituted by Prince Philip in 1978, on his twenty-fifth anniversary as Captain General of the Royal Marines.

THE COLOURS AND THE CORPS MOTTO

For all ceremonial parades each Commando has two Colours: the Queen's Colour and the Regimental Colour. For a member of the Royal family, or a visiting Head of State, the Queen's Colour is carried by a guard of honour. For other VIPs, the Regimental Colour is displayed.

The Queen's Colour carries the battle honour 'Gibraltar' above the crown, and the reigning monarch's cypher with foul anchor. Below is the globe and laurel wreath with the Corps motto: *Per Mare per Terram* – by sea, by land. (The orgins of the motto are obscure, but by all accounts it was first seen on the caps of Marines at the Battle of Bunker Hill in 1775.) All are superimposed on a Union Jack. The cords and tassels are gold interwoven with silks of the Commando's colour, which corresponds to its lanyard.

The Regimental Colour's centrepiece is similar to that of the Queen's Colour, with the exception of the cypher, which is that of George IV and has the number of the unit below the motto. The flag background is blue. At the pike head is the Union Jack with the Royal cypher at the four corners. The cords are similar to those of the Queen's Colour.

The Corps Colours

These are four-parts navy blue, one-part yellow, one-part green, two-parts red, and four-parts navy blue. The blue sections represent the naval connection, the yellow the colour of the Maritime Regiment's coats in 1664, the green the light infantry, and the red was the colour of the British infantry tunic prior to 1876. With some uniforms the Royal Marines wear a broad belt of heavy-duty material, woven in the Corps colours. The Royal Marines' tie is a combination of diagonal stripes in the Corps colours.

• The last man in the Royal Navy to be hanged from the yard-arm was Marine John Dallinger aboard HMS *Leven* in the River Yangtze, China, on 13 July 1860. Dallinger had been found guilty of two attempted murders.

• The youngest recorded British 'soldier' enlisted under the Army Act was Gunner Walter James Taylor, RMA. He enlisted on 27 August 1917 aged 13 years and 150 days. Meanwhile the youngest 'Old Contemptible' of the British Expeditionary Force in France in 1914 was Private Denis Robert Kearns, RMLI. He entered the Marines aged 14 years and 3 days and was disembarked in France on 26 August 1914, aged 14 years and 194 days.

• Perhaps the last duel in this country took place between Captain Alexander Seaton of the 11th Dragoons and Lieutenant Henry Hawkey of the Royal Marines on 20 May 1845 at Browndown near Gosport, over the attention that Seaton, a married officer, was paying to Hawkey's wife. In the resulting duel Seaton was mortally wounded and Hawkey tried for murder. Lieutenant Hawkey and Second Lieutenant Pym, RM were later acquitted at their trial, when it was proved that Seaton had died because of the surgery he had undergone and not from the wound that he had suffered during the duel.

• The record of Major Edward Nicolls during the Napoleonic Wars typified the service of his Corps. After being commissioned in 1795 he was in action 107 times, wounded six times, charged with Court Martial offences twice and became a full General in 1854, before his death in February 1865. He was known as 'Fighting Nicolls'.

• General Wolfe of Quebec was first commissioned as a Marine officer in 1741, and his father was Colonel of the regiment.

• The late Harry H. Corbett (of *Steptoe and Son*) served as a Royal Marine during the Second World War.

• The Scottish song 'Charlie is m' darling' was written by Captain Charles Gray of the Royal Marines in the early nineteenth century.

• In 1964 the Royal Marines were granted the privilege of remaining seated during the Loyal Toast.

• In April 1943 an unidentified corpse was dressed up to represent a Major William Martin, Royal Marines, an imaginary Intelligence Officer. Equipped with false papers, designed to mislead the Germans as to the whereabouts of the Allied landings in Europe, the body was thrown into the sea from HM Submarine *Seraph* and was later found on a Spanish beach. The great ruse was apparently successful and after the war the story was made into the film *The Man Who Never Was*.

• Perhaps the strangest story of all time concerns Hannah Snell, who under the name of James Gray disguised herself and joined the Marines at Portsmouth in 1745 in her quest to find her husband, who had deserted her. She embarked on the sloop *Swallow*, sailed to the East Indies and fought in the siege of Pondicherry in India, where she was wounded. Having discovered her husband had died, she took discharge and it was only then that she disclosed her sex, in spite of having been lashed earlier in her service and hiding a wound that would have disclosed her gender. She soon became a well-known figure of the time, after a brief stage career and while running a public house in Wapping called the 'Woman in Masquerade'.

Hannah Snell (after a painting now in the Royal Marines Museum)

Some Historical Facts

41 Cdo RM: formed in 1942 from men of 8th RM Bn for service in Second World War, disbanded but later reformed from time to time; served in Korea. Reformed in 1960 but disbanded May 1981.

43 Cdo RM: formed in 1943 from men of 2nd RM Bn and saw service in Second World War. Reformed in 1961, disbanded 1968.

44, 46, 47 and 48 RM Cdos: formed in 1943 and after service in Second World War were disbanded.

RM Artillery (RMA): formed in 1804 as artillery companies of the Corps and amalgamated with RMLI in 1923.

RM Light Infantry: from 1855 to 1923 the infantry arm was designated Light Infantry.

The Grand Divisions: the original Port establishments – Chatham, Portsmouth, Plymouth and Woolwich (1805–69). Became known as the Divisions until the reorganization of the Corps in 1947 into Groups.

The RM Division: formed in Second World War for amphibious ops, but re-mustered in 1943 as Cdos and LC crews.

MNBDOs: these Mobile Naval Base Defence Organizations were formed in Second World War from a nucleus of Royal Marines who had worked with LC, coast batteries and on installing guns in advance naval bases. Elements of MNBDO I provided the rearguard on Crete in 1941, before MNBDO I and II were disbanded to form LC flotillas, etc.

RMBPD: this Boom Patrol Detachment of swimmer-canoeists included the 'Cockleshell Heroes' who raided Bordeaux in 1942, and it was – with Detachment 385 – a forerunner of the SBS.

116 and 117 RM Bdes: formed in 1945 from LC crews and others for ops in the Pacific, but fought as infantry in NW Europe.

5 RM AA Bde: formed from AA Regts of the MNBDOs in 1944 for ops in NW Europe.

Honorary Appointments and the Commandant-General

The Captain General

In 1953 HM The Queen honoured the Corps by appointing HRH The Prince Philip, Duke of Edinburgh, as Captain General of the Royal Marines in succession to the late King George VI.

Colonels Commandant

HM The Queen may appoint four Colonels Commandant, honorary positions held for four years. They are usually retired RM Generals, but may be of equivalent rank from any service. For two years one of these is appointed Representative Colonel Commandant to carry out mainly formal duties. Colonels Commandant wear the uniform of a General with a Colonel's badges of rank.

From August 1965 until his death in August 1979, Admiral of the Fleet the Earl Mountbatten of Burma was Life Colonel Commandant of the Corps. His family had a long and proud association with the Royal Marines. During the Second World War, when the role of the Corps was in question, he ensured the commitment of Marines to Commando operations.

Honorary Colonel

On 5 May 1981, Crown Prince Harald of Norway was appointed an Honorary Colonel. He is the first member of a foreign Royal family to hold such an appointment in the Corps.

The Commandant-General

The senior general officer commanding the Corps is the Commandant-General (CGRM). He, like the Commanders-in-Chief Fleet and Naval Home Command, is responsible to the Admiralty Board. His Chief of Staff heads a Department which functions as both the staff of a Commander-in-Chief's headquarters and as part of the Defence and Naval Staff.

The Distinguished Flying Cross

Captain Jeffrey Niblett, RM

It was not until the Falklands War of 1982 that a Royal Marine received a DFC, and in the course of this conflict two were awarded, one to Captain Niblett the other to Lieutenant R.J. Nunn (posthumous), along with a Distinguished Flying Medal to Sergeant William C. O'Brien, all members of 3 Commando Brigade Air Squadron.

During the attack on Darwin and Goose Green, Captain Niblett led a section of two Scout helicopters for two days, supplying ammunition and evacuating casualties, often under fire. During one mission, both Scouts were sighted by Argentinian Pucara aircraft, which they initially managed to evade. One of the Scouts was then shot down, which placed the other, flown by Captain Niblett, under great threat. However, with exceptional skill he managed to evade three further cannon and rocket attacks to complete his mission safely, for which he was awarded a DFC.

VICTORIA CROSSES

Corporal John Pettyjohn: Crimea, 2 November 1854

John Pettyjohn was a labourer until, the day before his twenty-first birthday, he went to Plymouth and enlisted for unlimited service in the Royal Marines. He was born at Dean Prior, Buckfastleigh, near Ashburton in Devon on 11 June 1823.

He received his Victoria Cross for gallantry at the Battle of Inkerman. Having placed himself in an advanced position he successfully led his men in routing Russian marksmen from some caves. Promoted to Colour Sergeant, Corporal Pettyjohn was discharged from the Marines on 16 June 1865, after twenty-one years and six days' service. During this time he had spent sixteen years and ninety-four days either at sea or in foreign stations. He died aged sixty-two, and was buried in the Southern Cemetery, Manchester. He was married and had two daughters.

Bombardier Thomas Wilkinson, RMA: Crimea, 5 June 1855

Thomas Wilkinson was born at Marygate, Yorkshire in 1831. He was the fourteenth recipient of the Victoria Cross, which he received from Queen Victoria at a Hyde Park ceremony on 26 June 1857.

While under heavy fire, during the bombardment of Sebastopol, calling on his comrades for help, Bombardier Wilkinson repaired the damage to his guns position.

He was discharged 'invalided' from the Royal Marine Artillery on 12 October 1859. He was twenty-eight years old. He died in York aged fifty-five of exhaustion and diarrhoea. He was also awarded the French Legion of Honour.

Lieutenant George Dare Dowell, RMA: Viborg, Baltic Sea, 13 July 1855

George Dare Dowell was born at Fishbourne, Chichester, in Sussex, on 15 February 1831. Educated at the Royal Naval School, New Cross, London, he joined the Royal Marines as a Second Lieutenant on 25 July 1848. He transferred to the Royal Marine Artillery on 18 July 1849. On 6 October 1851 he was promoted First Lieutenant.

Following an explosion in a rocket boat of the *Arrogant* during the Crimean War (1853–56), Lieutenant Dowell, who was at the time on board the *Ruby*, jumped into one of the *Ruby*'s boats and, with three volunteers, while under heavy fire from the enemy, went to the assistance of the men in the stricken boat. Having rescued three of the crew, he returned to the boat and managed to

save that also. He married the daughter of a Colonel and had a family of nine, five sons and four daughters. When he retired with the rank of Lieutenant-Colonel, he emigrated to New Zealand. He died on 3 August 1910, aged seventy-nine. His was a blue ribbon Victoria Cross, denoting that it was gained at sea.

Captain Lewis Stratford Tollemache Halliday, RMLI: Boxer Rebellion, 24 June 1900

Lewis Halliday was born at Medway House, Hampshire, on 14 May 1870 into a military family, and was commissioned into the Royal Marine Light Infantry, as a Second Lieutenant, on 1 September 1889.

On 24 June 1900 the enemy, consisting of Boxers and Imperial troops, fiercely attacked the west wall of the British Legation in Peking, setting fire to the west gate of the south stable quarters, and taking cover in nearby buildings. As the fire spread, the Imperial troops continued their attack, making it impossible for the inhabitants to contain the spreading fire. Leading a party of twenty Marines through a hole in the Legation wall, Captain Halliday began attacking the enemy. He was shot at close range, the bullet fracturing his left shoulder and penetrating part of his lung. He continued fighting, regardless of the severity of his wounds, calling on his Marines to 'carry on and not mind him'. Unaided, he walked back to the hospital, refusing all help in case it reduced the numbers involved in the attack. He was awarded the Victoria Cross on 1 January 1901, twenty-one days before the death of Queen Victoria. He was appointed Adjutant General, Royal Marines on 1 October 1927, being promoted to General while holding the appointment. Prior to his retirement in October 1930, he was awarded the KCB. He was appointed the Deputy Lieutenant for Devon, and Gentleman Usher to the Sword of State. He died at Dorking, Surrey on 9 March 1966, aged ninety-six.

Lance Corporal Walter Richard Parker, RMLI: Gallipoli, 1 May 1915

Walter Richard Parker was born in Grantham, Lincolnshire on 20 September 1881. After school, in London's Kentish Town, he went to work at Stanton Ironworks as a coremaker. On 9 September 1914 he joined the Royal Marines as a short-service recruit in Nottingham, and was posted to the Portsmouth Division.

On the night of 10 April 1915, somewhere near Gaba Tepe, Lance Corporal Parker volunteered to be a stretcher-bearer, along with a relief party detailed to carry stores, medical supplies and ammunition, to a trench where some forty men and a number of wounded were in difficulty. There had been several casualties in previous attempts to take the supplies to the troops in the cut-off trench. As there were no connecting trenches, the only way to reach the beleaguered men was across 400 yards of open ground controlled by enemy rifle fire.

Alone and in daylight – all the water and ammunition carriers had been either killed or wounded – he reached the isolated men and managed to give what assistance he could to the wounded. It is reported that he displayed extreme courage and remained cool and collected under very trying circumstances. In the early morning of the following day the trench had to be evacuated and Lance Corporal Parker helped to remove and attend to the wounded although, during this operation, he was seriously wounded himself. The report on Parker continued: 'During the three previous days he displayed consistent bravery and energy whilst in charge of the battalion stretcher-bearers...In nearly every case the wounded had to be evacuated over exposed ground which was under fire.'

Suffering from brain fever, he was discharged from the service in June 1916. He was presented with a marble and gilt clock, inscribed by the officers and men of his division. He also received a war gratuity of £10. Olive, his wife, was presented with a brooch. It appears that he spent the remainder of the war in a munitions factory. He never recovered from his wounds, and he died at Stapleford, Nottingham, on 28 November 1936. He was fifty-five years old.

Major Francis John William Harvey, RMLI: HMS *Lion*, Battle of Jutland, 31 May 1916

Francis Harvey was born in Sydenham, the son of a Navy Commander, on 19 April 1873. His military education was at Sandhurst and Dartmouth, and on 1 July 1893 he was promoted to Second Lieutenant in the Royal Marine Light Infantry. Following various shore-based and seagoing appointments, he joined the battle cruiser HMS *Lion* on 12 February 1913.

During the Battle of Jutland Major Harvey commanded 'Q' turret, containing two 13½-inch guns situated between the second and third funnels of the ship. A 12-inch shell from the *Lutzow* penetrated 'Q' turret and exploded. Severely injured, Major Harvey ordered the magazine doors to be closed and the area flooded. The enemy shell caused havoc in the immediate area, and of the sixty or so serving in that part of the ship, only three survived. Later that night Major Harvey's badly burned body was found. He was buried at sea on 15 September 1916. The Victoria Cross was presented to his widow by King George V on 29 November 1916.

Major Frederick William Lumsden, DSO, RMA: Western Front, April 1917

Frederick William Lumsden was born at Frizbad, India, on 14 December 1872. His father was a civil servant in India. Like most expatriates, Frederick Lumsden's family sent him to England to be educated, in his case, Bristol Grammar School. After school he entered the Royal Marines, and was promoted to full Lieutenant on 1 July 1891. He specialized in signalling, musketry gunnery and German. In the New Year's honours list of 1 January 1917 he was awarded the Distinguished Service Order.

Major Lumsden was awarded his Victoria Cross for successfully retrieving six enemy field guns which were under constant fire from the enemy. He personally led his recovery teams through a barrage of hostile fire to recover the field guns. Without any regard for his own personal safety, he continued with the operation, making several sorties under worsening conditions, to obtain his objective. In addition to his Victoria Cross, Major Lumsden was awarded three bars to his DSO for conspicuous gallantry.

He was also awarded the CB in the King's Birthday Honours for 1918, although it appears he did not live to hear of it, as he was killed on the night of 3 June 1918. He was shot through the head as his position came under attack. He lies buried in the Berles New Military Cemetery in France.

He was in addition awarded the Belgian Croix de Guerre, and was four times Mentioned in Despatches. Outside the Royal Marines Museum, Eastney, there is a memorial to Brigadier-General Lumsden, VCS, DSO, CdeG.

Captain Edward Bamford, DSO, RMLI: Zeebrugge, 23 April 1918

Edward Bamford was born the son of a Church of England clergyman, in Highgate, London, on 28 May 1887. Like several other Marine officers he was educated at Sherborne, and entered the Royal Marines on 1 September 1905. His Victoria Cross citation reads:

This officer landed on the mole from the *Vindictive*, with numbers 5, 7 and 8 platoons of the Marine storming force, in the face of great difficulties. When on the mole, and under heavy fire, he displayed the greatest initiative in the command of his company, and by his total disregard of danger showed a magnificent example to his men. He first established a strong point on the right of the disembarkation and, when satisfied that was safe, led an assault on a battery to the left with the utmost coolness and valour ...

While on duty in the South China Sea he became ill and died, on board HMS *Cumberland*, on 30 September 1928. He was buried in the English cemetery in Shanghai. He was aged forty-one.

In addition to his Victoria Cross and Distinguished Service Order, he was awarded the Russian Order of St Anne 3rd Class with Swords, the French Legion of Honour, and the Japanese Order of the Rising Sun 4th Class, in recognition for services rendered on the occasion of the visit of the Crown Prince of Japan to England in 1921.

Sergeant Norman Augustus Finch, RMA: Zeebrugge, 23 April 1918

Norman Finch was born on 26 December 1890 in Handsworth, Birmingham. For a time, after leaving school, he was a toolmaker and machinist, before enlisting in the Royal Marine Artillery on 15 January 1908.

After numerous postings, including a China tour, he was promoted to Sergeant and found himself taking part in the Zeebrugge operation in April 1918. Sergeant Finch was second in command of the pompoms and Lewis guns in the foretop of HMS *Vindictive*. His ship came under heavy fire from the enemy and splinters from the superstructure were causing casualties. Sergeant Finch and his crew maintained constant fire with their weapons, minimizing the enemy's return fire. During the exchange of fire, two heavy shells made direct hits on the foretop. With the exception of Sergeant Finch, all were killed. Although wounded, and in an exposed position, Sergeant Finch located a Lewis gun and continued firing, harassing the enemy on the mole. The foretop received another direct hit. According to his citation, before the top was destroyed Sergeant Finch had done invaluable work, and by his bravery had undoubtedly saved many lives. King George V presented the Victoria Cross to him on 31 July 1918 at Buckingham Palace. He was discharged from the Royal Marines on 26 December 1929, after twenty-one years' service. He received an £86 pension payment, and earned three good conduct badges during his service.

He held several civilian appointments, including postman, bank messenger and Yeoman of the Guard. With the impending hostilities in Europe, he re-entered the Marines and was promoted to the rank of Temporary Lieutenant serving as a stores officer. He was finally released from service in August 1945. Aged seventy-four, he became Divisional Sergeant-Major in Her Majesty's Bodyguard of the Yeoman of the Guard and was awarded the Royal Victorian Medal for his services. He died in Saint Mary's Hospital, Portsmouth on 15 March 1966.

Corporal Thomas Peck Hunter, 43 Commando: Lake Comacchio, 3 April 1945

Thomas Hunter was born on 6 October 1923 in the garrison town of Aldershot in Hampshire. After school in Edinburgh he became an apprentice stationer. When war broke out he was for a time a member of the local Home Guard. He was conscripted for military service on 8 May 1942 and enlisted in the Royal Marines as a 'Hostilities Only' Marine.

After amphibious training he was assigned to 43 Royal Marine Commando and took part in further training at Achnacarry in Scotland. During his training he became an expert shot with a rifle and light machine-gun. On 9 January 1944, 43 Commando disembarked at Castellano to take part in the Italian Campaign. On 3 April 1945, during the Battle of Lake Comacchio, he was killed after offering himself as a target in order to save his troop. An account of the events reads:

In Italy during the advance of the Commando to its final objective, Corporal Hunter of 'C' Troop was in charge of a Bren group of the leading sub-section of the Commando. Having advanced to within 400 yards of the canal, he observed the enemy were holding a group of houses south of the canal.

Realizing that his Troop behind him were devoid of cover, and that the enemy would cause heavy casualties as soon as they opened fire, Corporal Hunter seized the Bren gun and charged alone across 200 yards of open ground. The Spandaus from the houses, and at least six from the north bank of the canal, opened fire and at the same time enemy mortars started to fire at the Troop. Corporal Hunter attracted most of the fire, and so determined was his charge and his firing from the hip that the enemy in the houses became demoralized. Showing complete disregard for the intense enemy fire, he ran through the houses, changing magazines as he ran, and alone cleared the houses. Six Germans surrendered to him, and the remainder fled across a footbridge, or to the north bank of the canal.

The Troop dashing up behind Corporal Hunter now became the target for all the Spandaus on the north of the canal. Again, offering himself as a target, he lay in full view of the enemy on a heap of rubble, and fired at the concrete pillboxes on the other side. He again drew most of the fire, but by now the greater part of his Troop had made for the safety of the houses. During this period he shouted encouragement to the remainder, and called only for more Bren magazines with which to engage the enemy. Firing with great accuracy up to the last, Corporal Hunter was finally hit in the head by a burst of Spandau fire and killed instantly.

There can be no doubt that Corporal Hunter offered himself as a target in order to save his Troop, and only the speed of his movement prevented him from being hit earlier. The skill and accuracy with which he used the Bren gun is proved by the way he demoralized the enemy and later did definitely silence many of the Spandaus firing on his Troop as they crossed the open ground, so much so, that under his covering fire elements of the Troop made their final objective before he was killed. Throughout the operation his magnificent courage, leadership and cheerfulness had been an inspiration to all his comrades. *London Gazette*, 8 June 1945

Corporal Thomas Peck Hunter was buried at the Argenta Gap War Cemetery in Italy. At a private investiture in the Palace of Holyroodhouse his parents were presented with his Victoria Cross by King George V on 26 September 1945. In his home town of Stenhouse, Edinburgh, eight houses were dedicated to his memory.

WEAPONS

Weapons used by 3 Commando Brigade, RM

A Platoon Weapons
SLR – Self Loading Rifle

SA 80 – IW and LSW – Individual and Light Support Weapon

GPMG – General Purpose Machine Gun (light role and SF role)

LMG 6 Light Machine Gun – still employed in various theatres

9mm Browning Pistol

AR15 – (M16, used mainly by ML Cadres)

SMG – Sub Machine Gun (to be phased out), Stirling 2-inch Mortar (being replaced by 51mm mortar)

66mm LAW – Light Anti-tank Weapon

84mm MAW – Medium Anti-tank Weapon

LAW 80 – Light Anti-tank Weapon – will replace 66mm LAW and 84mm MAW

L42 Sniper's Rifle

Heckler and Koch SMG (Special forces only)

Ingram Machine Pistol (Special forces only)

Remington 'Wingmaster' Shotgun – certain theatres only

Federal Riot Gun – Internal Security only

B Grenades
L2 Grenade – HE

80 Grenade – Phosphorus

C Support/Heavy Weapons
81mm Mortar

Milan Anti-tank Missile

Anti-aircraft Missile – now replaced by Javelin

105 Light Gun (29 Cdo Regt RA)

Rapier

Javelin – to replace Anti-aircraft Missile

Stinger Anti-aircraft (RNLMC attached 3 Cdo Bde)

Dragon Anti-tank (RNLMC attached 3 Cdo Bde)

Lt/Med Recce Sqd Scimitar 30mm Cannon
Scorpion 76mm Gun

COMMANDO TESTS

These are the final tests that every man must successfully complete in order to win a green beret. They are undertaken in full battle-order kit weighing 30 lbs (2 st. 2 lbs), and probably at least 40 lbs (2 st. 12 lbs) when wet. Additionally, each man will be carrying a rifle weighing just under 10 lbs.

Tarzan Course	5 minutes for recruits, 4.5 minutes for YOs (Young Officers)
Tarzan Course and Assault Course	13 minutes for recruits, 12.5 minutes for YOs
Endurance Course, plus 4-mile run back to camp	73 minutes for recruits, 70 minutes for YOs
9-mile speed march	90 minutes for all
6-mile speed march	60 minutes for all
30-mile yomp	8 hours for recruits, 7 hours for YOs
30-foot rope climb	no time limit
Battle Swimming Test	no time limit – the man jumps into a pool wearing full kit, swims for fifty metres, treads water for two minutes, takes off kit and hands it to a man standing at the side of the pool and treads water for another two minutes. At no time can he touch the side of the pool.

NB After the 9-mile speed march the men must take part in a troop attack. After the Endurance Course and run-back they must be able to fire their rifles on the 25-metre range immediately – this is as much a test of a man's ability to keep his rifle clean as it is of his fitness and stamina.

MARINESPEAK

Most communities establish their own phrases and expressions; with the passing of time, a separate language may develop that can be understood only by their members. The language of the Geordie and the Cockney, for example, is barely comprehensible to anyone living in Sussex or Dorset, which also have regional vocabularies. Prisoners, doctors, pilots, the police and the military all have their own languages, which most outsiders fail to understand. It is all part of man's inherent tribalism, and the need for security and companionship which compels him to form a bond within a select community. He feels that knowing the language of a community gains him social acceptance and a place within its society.

So it is with the Royal Marines, who over the years have developed their own 'language', most of it derived, as one would expect, from Royal Navy terms and expressions. Marinespeak is believed to have several hundred words and phrases. Here are a few of them, extracted from the book *Jackspeak* by Surgeon Commander R.T. Jolly, OBE.

Ace	Something that is first-class.
Acquire	A barely legal method of obtaining an item which may be in short supply.
Adrift	Late for duty.
Agony Bags	Bagpipes.
Amen Wallah	A padre or chaplain. Other terms are: Sky Pilot, Devil Dodger, Bible Basher, Holy Joe.
Ashore	Anywhere that is not on the ship. 'We had a good run ashore last night.'
Bandy	Any member of the Royal Marines' Band Service.
Barracks	Any part of a naval ship allocated to the Royal Marines.
Beasting	Heavy physical training. It can also imply bullying by NCOs.
Benny	Slang term for a Falkland Islander, also referred to as a kelper.
Bin	To get rid of, or abandon something, usually a project, but individuals can also be 'binned', implying that they have failed the course.
Bivvy	An abbreviation of bivouac shelter. Either a small military tent or one man-made from the natural surroundings.
Bronzy Time	Sunbathing.
Cab	A helicopter.
Call for Hughie	To vomit.
Cam out	To apply camouflage cream to the face and hands.
Cherryberry	A member of the Parachute Regiment.
Clag	Poor weather, low cloud affecting visibility.
Clanger	A badly timed remark that is sufficiently embarrassing to make the ship's bell clang.
Dhobi	Possibly an Indian or Arabic word used to refer to laundry and clothes washing.
Dicked	To be soundly beaten, usually in a sporting event.
Dip	A general-purpose word meaning that someone has failed a course or exam.
Dockyard Matey	Nickname for dockyard workers.
Donk	A petrol or diesel engine.
Dummy Run	A rehearsal for a military exercise without a shot being fired.
Ear Pounding	Verbal criticism.
Egyptian PT	Sleep.
Elmer	General term for an American. Full expression: Elmer J. Chickenshit Junior.
Embuggerance Factor	Something that does not contribute to the ease of operation.
Endex	End of exercise.
Essence	Indicating beauty. 'She's essence.'
Fanny Rat	A ladies' man or womanizer.
Figgy Duff	Any stodgy or suet-based pudding.
First Drill	The senior NCO at Lympstone responsible for all ceremonial drill.
Fish's Tit	Couldn't care less. 'I couldn't give a fish's tit.'
Flakers	Dead tired.
Foo-foo	Talcum powder. Pusser's Foo-foo is a foot and body powder issued for the tropics.
Gannet	A Marine who eats quickly and often.
Gash	Anybody or anything considered useless. It also refers to all rubbish on board ship.
Globe & Bustard	Crest of the Royal Marines or the *Globe & Laurel* magazine.
Gobbling Rods	Eating utensils.

Grab-a-Granny Night	Regular evening at the local dance hall when the more mature ladies attend and 'Royal' is assured of the action he seeks.
Grot	A cabin or room, personalized by the owner.
Heads	The ship's toilets.
Heap	Individual of poor personal appearance.
Honkers	Hong Kong.
Horlicks	The alternative to 'cock-up'. 'He made a right horlicks of something or other.'
Hot Bunking	When sleeping accommodation is limited, several Marines alternatively using the same bunk when coming off duty.
Howling	Drunk.
Icers	Cold. 'The weather is icers outside.'
Ickies	Foreign currency; Ickie Store refers to a bank.
Immaculate	Relating to anything that is of high quality.
Ish	Several meanings; most common usage: a full issue of equipment. 'That is the complete ish.'
It's only pain!	Frequently heard by recruits during training at Lympstone as 'encouragement' to get on with it and do better.
Jack	Sailor of the Royal Navy.
Jack it in	To give up.
Jenny	Jenny Wren, a member of the Women's Royal Naval Service.
Jesus Nut	The system which secures a helicopter's rotor blade on to the drive shaft.
Jolly	A Royal Marine (from Rudyard Kipling). Can also mean a pleasant trip that has no real purpose.
Juniors	The Junior Command Course, compulsory for any Marine wishing to be promoted to Corporal.
Kag	Unwanted equipment. 'Leave it, it's a lot of kag.'
Kit Muster	Inspection of a Marine's full issue of clothing and personal equipment.
Klicks	Kilometers.
Knacker	Referring to a person being overweight.
Knocker	Nickname for anyone with the surname White.
Knuckle	To knuckle under means to get down to work and complete the task.
Leatherneck	A member of the United States Marine Corps. Note: the best candidate passing out from the Juniors' Course at Lympstone each year is awarded the Leatherneck Trophy.
Leg it	To run away. Can also be used when there is no transport available and you have to walk. An ideal pair of running shoes for a Marine would be a pair of Nike Leggits!
Limers	A soft drink, usually prepared from a powder mix.
Loggies	A member of the RM Commando Logistics Regiment.
Looney Juice	Sometimes called loopy juice, referring to any form of strong drink.
Lovats	The number two service dress of the Royal Marines.
Madhouse	The Ministry of Defence – London.
Mankey	Something filthy or dirty.
MoD Plod	A member of the Ministry of Defence police.
Most Dangerous Thing in the World	Pre-1982, Jolly Jack (a sailor) with a rifle. Post-Falklands, an officer with a map!
Muck or Nettles	Little choice between two unpleasant alternatives. 'Take your pick, it's either muck or nettles.'
Muster	When a kit inspection is regarded to have been up to standard requirements.
NAAFI	The organization which operates service shops and canteens is the Navy, Army and Air Force Institutes.
Nause	Any problem with a civilian authority about permission to do something or other.
Neaters	Undiluted rum.
Neck Oil	Beer; any strong beverage to get down your neck for internal lubrication.
Nod/Noddy	A Royal Marine recruit.
Nutty	Confectionery.
Oggie	A Cornish pasty, or anyone born in Cornwall.

On your Jack (Jones)	Alone.
Oppo	A close friend within the unit.
Other Half	A figure of speech when drinking, implying that you should have another one.
Out of his Tree	Referring to doubting someone's sanity. 'If he thinks I am going to do that, then he's out of his tree.'
Outside	Civilian life. Life beyond the Marines.
Party	A female.
Pash	A female with whom a Marine has formed a strong relationship.
Pension Trap	A reluctance to become involved in anything that may endanger your pension as you are nearing the end of your service career.
Percy Pongo	A soldier. Derived from the firm belief by Marines that those in the Army do not wash frequently.
Phot	A photographer, usually naval, but can be used for civilian and media photographers.
Pusser	One of the most used words in Marinespeak, referring to any item, or person for that matter, that is a Navy item. For example: Pusser's Crabfat: thick, warship-grey paint. Pusser's Daps: white plimsoll shoes. Pusser's Dust: cheap instant coffee. Pusser's Loaf: a biscuit. Pusser's Dip: a candle.
Rack out	To go to sleep.
Rag-bag	Untidy person.
Ratpack	A ration pack.
RHIP	'Rank has its privileges' – a way of deferring to a senior officer.
Rock-all	Nothing.
Run Ashore	Recreation away from the ship or barracks.
Schoolie	Schoolmaster, educational officer, instruction officer.
Scran	Food.
Scratcher	A bed.
Seagulls	Any group of (Army) Guards or Cavalry officers' wives talking among themselves.
Shitehawk	General term of abuse.
Shreds/Shredies	Underpants.
'Tell that to the Marines'	When flying fish were being described to the Court of Charles I, it is reported that a Captain of Marines confirmed the traveller's story. The Monarch's response was that in future, when a story needed confirmation, his Marines would do the job!
Thickers	Condensed milk.
Thumb in bum, mind in neutral	The description of someone who is day-dreaming while working, and not paying attention.
Tickler	Cigarette, usually self-rolled, from a tin of ticklers.
Trap	To acquire a female on a run ashore.
Truckie	A member of the Royal Corps of Transport.
Twat Hat	A soft tweed hat with an all-round brim.
Ulu	A Malay word for jungle, sometimes written incorrectly as ooloo; now used to describe any remote location.
Up Homers	To be invited into a home.
Up Sticks	To strike camp and start yomping.
Up the Line	To travel away from base.
Up to Speed	Fully aware of the facts surrounding the situation. 'Are you up to speed on the new regulations?'
Wah-Wah	A cavalry officer – based on the noise that a group of them make in conversation.
Wellies from the Queen	Free contraceptives.
Wet	To have a drink.
Whinge	Complain, moan.
Wrap	To stop or give up.
Write-off	Useless.
Yaffle	To eat hurriedly.
Yeti	A spectacular fall on skis.
Yomp	Forced march with a heavy load.
Yo-yo	Young officer in training at Lympstone.

FREEDOMS

Deal
The Freedom of the Borough of Deal was bestowed on the Corps in February 1945. A Royal Marine appears in the Borough's coat of arms.

Chatham
The Freedom of Chatham was bestowed on the Corps in December 1949, prior to the Marine barracks being closed.

Plymouth
The Corps received the Freedom of the City in May 1955 to mark the 200th anniversary of its association with the people of Plymouth.

Portsmouth
The Captain General received the Freedom of the City on behalf of the Corps in May 1959.

Exmouth
The Corps was adopted by the Exmouth Urban District Council in May 1968 and has been re-affirmed by the new Borough.

Poole
In September 1973 the Corps became the Honorary Freeman of the Borough and County of the town of Poole.

The City of London
Contrary to popular belief, the Royal Marines have never been awarded the Freedom of the City of London. However, the Corps was affiliated to the Church of St Lawrence Jewry, Guildhall, on 23 April 1974.

Stanley, Falkland Islands
The Freedom of Stanley was bestowed on the Corps in December 1976.

Medway
After the creation of the new Borough of Medway, the Royal Marines were admitted as Honorary Freemen in May 1979.

Newcastle
The Royal Marines were awarded the Freedom of the City of Newcastle on 25 November 1989.

ASSOCIATIONS WITH LIVERY COMPANIES

Worshipful Company of Armourers and Brasiers makes an annual award to the Royal Marine who achieves the best results on the Armourers 3 course.

The Honourable Company of Master Mariners adopted the Royal Marines Reserve (City of London) in 1953.

Worshipful Company of Stationers and Papermakers adopted the Corps in 1949, and the 1952 stand of Colours of 45 Commando are laid up in Stationers' Hall, London.

SELECT BIBLIOGRAPHY

Blumberg, General Sir H.E., KCB, RM, *Royal Marines Records Part 3, 1837/1914* (published by The Royal Marines Historical Society, 1982).

Edgeworth, Anthony and St Jorre, John de, *The Marines* (Sidgwick & Jackson, 1989).

Field, Col. C., *Britain's Sea Soldiers* (Lyceum Press, 1924).

Foster, Nigel, *The Making of a Royal Marine Commando* (Sidgwick, 1987).

Fowler, William, *The Royal Marines (1956–1984)* (Osprey – Men at Arms Series).

Globe & Laurel (Journal of the Royal Marines) (1987–90).

Ladd, James B., *Assault from the Sea* (David & Charles, 1976).

Royal Marine Commando (Hamlyn, 1982).

Lockhart, Sir Robert Hamilton Bruce, *The Marines Were There* (Putnam, 1950).

Marsh, A.E., *Flying Marines* (1980).

Phillips, Lucas C.E., *The Cockleshell Heroes* (Heinemann, 1956).

The Royal Marines Museum, *The Story of Britain's Sea Soldiers*.

Smith, Peter and Oakley, Derek, *The Royal Marines: A Pictorial History* (Spellmount Ltd, 1989).

Thompson, Leroy, *British Commandos in Action* (Squadron, Signal Publications Inc., 1987).

Trendell, John, *Operation Music Maker: The Story of Royal Marines Bands* (published privately, 1988).

SOURCES FOR THE HISTORICAL SECTION

Jolly, Surgeon Commander R.T., OBE, *Jackspeak: The Pusser's Guide to Royal Navy and Royal Marines Slang* (published privately, 1988).

Ladd, James D., *Royal Marines of the 1970s and 1980s* (pamphlet published by the Dept of the Commandant-General Royal Marines). (The Military Background, Royal Marines Organization, Royal Marines School of Music's Organization, Honorary Appointments and the Commandant-General, Regimental Music, Some Historical Facts, The Colours and the Corps Motto, Uniforms of the Royal Marines, Freedoms.)

The Royal Marine Victoria Crosses (Royal Marines Museum). Royal Marines Museum Catalogue. (The Marens, Unusual Facts, The Distinguished Flying Cross.)

PHOTOGRAPHIC NOTES

During the past twenty-five years or so, my photographic equipment has changed little. I use Leica cameras exclusively. Leitz lenses are the world's finest: their robust mounts and superb optics provide me with sparkling images that are without rival.

Leica bodies – I use both rangefinder and SLRs – are exquisitely designed to fit snugly in the hand. They are a true 'miniature' camera.

As foreign travel becomes increasingly fraught with problems, with scanners, searches and the ever-present thief, I keep my working equipment to a minimum, carried in innocuous-looking bags and cases.

Usually I carry two R6 bodies, with no more than six lenses ranging from 16mm to 400mm. A typical selection might be: 16mm, 24mm, 35mm, 90mm, 180mm and 400mm. On longer trips, where weight is critical, my prime optics would be replaced with the short and long zooms. An M6 with 21mm, 35mm and 50mm F1:4 Summilux would be tucked away in one of the large pockets of a shoulder bag.

Scattered throughout my luggage I carry polarizing filters, a small Leica tabletop tripod, cable release, Swiss Army knife, watchmaker's screwdrivers, miniature tape recorder, tapes, a collection of pens and a large notebook. Film is a question of weather, and the atmosphere I wish to create within the book. I do not allow myself to be controlled by any specific brand.

INDEX

Aden, 8, 125, 129
administration: WRNS, 27–8
Admiralty, 93
Admiralty Interview Board (AIB), 136–40
Air Squadron, 48–53
Aladdin RM, 118–20
Albert Hall, London, 114
All Arms Commando Course, 25
Anglo-Dutch Wars (1665), 8
Anglo-Irish Agreement (1985), 14
Antarctica, 85–8
Arctic warfare, 72–9, 158
Argentina, 85, 131, 154
Army, 136, 159
Army Air Corps, 50, 52
Army Staff College, Camberley, 125, 127
assault courses, 43
auditions: musicians, 108–10
awards, 50

badges, 174, 181
Bahrain Defence Force, 112
Band Masters, 110–12
Band Sergeants, 105
Barnfield Theatre, Exeter, 118–20
Beating Retreat, 90–7
Beechmount Estate, Belfast, 19, 23
Belfast, 7, 12–24, 28, 39
Belize, 156
berets, 7, 33
Bessheim, Lake, 76–8
Beverley, Lieutenant-General Henry York La Roche, 124–5
Beverley, Sally, 125
blacks, 105–8, 157
Bland, Humphrey, 94
boat people: Hong Kong, 61, 66
boats: Fast Patrol Craft, 66–8, 69
Boer War, 97
boots, 36
Bordeaux, 149
Borneo, 127
Boxer Uprising, 8
brass bands, 101–15
Brigade Air Squadron (BAS), 48–53

Brighton, 32
Britannia, 85, 109
British Open Helicopter Championships, 50
'buddy system', 36, 40
Buenos Aires, 154
buglers, 110

Camberley, 127
Camel Company, 8
Canberra, 156
Canton, 60, 61, 62
Captain General, 177
Carlisle, 36
Causeway Bay, 60
cemeteries: Falklands, 85, 88
Cenotaph, 105
chaplains, 25–6
China, 60, 61, 62, 66–8, 69
Christmas pantomime, 116–20
Churchill, Sir Winston, 8
'The Cockleshell Heroes', 8, 149–50
Cold War, 7, 73, 157
Colonels Commandant, 177
Colour Sergeants, 144
Colours, 175
Commando tests, 183
Commando Training Centre Royal Marines (CTCRM), Lympstone, 33–47, 118, 125, 136–40
Cooper, Malcolm, 56
Corporals, 144, 156
Crimea, 8
Cross Furzes, 141
Crossmaglen, 12
Cyprus, 8, 125, 127, 158

Dartmoor, 33, 40, 41, 56, 141
Dartmouth, 136
Dawlish, 33
Deal, 40, 101–2, 103–14, 150
Department of Public Works, 93, 96
Devon, 33, 39
Dieppe Barracks, Sembawang, 50
Dieppe Raid, 8, 82, 127

Distinguished Flying Cross, 50, 168, 178
Divis Flats, Belfast, 22–3
divorce, 27
Dorset, 150
Dover, 103
Drake, Sir Francis, 102
Drill Sergeants, 110
drug-enforcement agencies, 158
Drum Majors, 110
Dutch Marine Corps, 158

Earls Court, 105
Eastbourne, 105
Eastney Barracks, 40, 128, 150
Edward, Prince, 8, 159–60
Egypt, 8
élitism, 134–5
Elizabeth II, Queen, 109, 125, 127, 129
Endurance, HMS, 85–6
endurance courses, 43
Eton, 134
Exe estuary, 33
Exeter, 118–20
Exmoor, 40, 41
Exmouth, 33

Falkland Islands, 82–8, 158
Falkland Islands Police, 154
Falklands War, 7, 16, 39, 50–2, 80–8, 129, 131, 154, 156, 157
Falls Road, Belfast, 20
Fast Patrol Craft (FPC), 66–8, 69
Flaud, René, 149
flying, 50–3
food, 40
Foreign Office, 93
Fort Halliday, 62
40 Commando, 127, 129, 156
42 Commando, 16–23, 125, 131
45 Commando, 129
France, 8, 50, 102, 103, 149
Frankton, Operation, 149–50
freedoms, 187
Freeland, Lieutenant-General Sir Ian, 16

French Revolutionary Wars, 8

Gallagh, John, 14
Garrod, Lady, 126, 127
Garrod, Lieutenant-General Sir
  Martin, 68, 126–7
Gazelle helicopters, 50, 52
Generals, 122–31
George II, King, 94
Gestapo, 28
Gibraltar, 96, 156
Gironde River, 149
Glasgow, 36
Goose Green, 16
Gosport, 136
Gray, General, 158
green berets, 7, 33
Greenwich, 136
Guards, 135, 144, 149, 152
Gurkhas, 131

Hampshire, 50, 128, 136
Harriers, 50
Harriet, Mount, 131
Harrow, 134
Hasler, Major 'Blondie', 149
helicopters, 50–2, 76, 131, 159
Hollywood, 37
Hong Kong, 58–69, 158, 159
Horn of Africa, 158
Horse Guards Parade, 93–7
House of Commons, 149
House of Lords, 149, 152
Household Brigade, 134

Ice Patrol, 85
immigrants: Hong Kong, 61, 66
India, 158
instructors, 38–9
instruments, musical, 114
intelligence: Northern Ireland,
  22–3
Inverness, 36
Iran, 158
Ireland, 8, 9–24, 27, 50, 125, 127,
  131, 135
Irish Republican Army (IRA),
  19–24, 101
Islamic fundamentalism, 158
Israel, 129

Jane (Wren), 27–8
Japan, 8

'K' Company 42 Commando,
  16–23
Kai Tak airport, Hong Kong, 62
Kent, 103
Kent, Mount, 156
Kent, William, 94
King's Squad, 47
Kirtley, John, 151–2
kit, 35, 36
Kowloon, 60

L96A1 sniper rifles, 56
lanyard, 175
Lee Enfield rifles, 56
library, music, 112–14
Lieutenants, 141, 146–7
Lillehammer, 76
Liverpool, 36
livery companies, 187
living allowances, 78
London, 60, 90–7
Longdon, Mount, 85
Lower Falls, Belfast, 19
Lyme Bay, 33
Lympstone, 25, 26, 32, 33–47,
  118, 136–40, 146, 156
Lynx helicopters, 50, 52
Lynx skidoos, 76–8

M-40A1 sniper rifles, 56
Malaya, 8, 127
Malta, 8, 125, 127, 129
Manchu Empire, 61
Manhattan Island, 60
Mao Tse-tung, 7
Marens, 169
Marines Museum, 150
Marinespeak, 37, 184–6
marksmen, 56
marriage, 27
Maudinaud brothers, 149
MI5, 22
Middle East, 158
Middle Wallop, 50, 52
military bands, 96–7, 101–15
Mill Hill Barracks, 125
Ministry of Defence, 79
Mitchell, Rear-Admiral, 103
Montevideo, 154
Montgomery, Field Marshal, 125,
  157
Moody Brook, 85
Morris, Dave, 153–4
motto, 175

Mountbatten, Earl, 150, 177
Mountbatten family, 97, 177
music library, 112–14
musicians, 68, 96–7, 98–115

NAAFI, 37, 40, 43, 64
Napoleonic Wars, 8
NATO, 72–4, 125, 158
Naval Air Station, Yeovilton, 52
Naval Party 8901, 85
NCOs, 8, 35, 142–7, 152, 156
Nelson, Lord, 102–3
Netherlands, 102, 103
New Territories, 60
New York, 60
New Zealand, 125
Newcastle, 36
Normandy landings, 8
North Africa, 129
North Howard Street Mill, Belfast,
  14–19
Northern Ireland, 8, 9–24, 27, 50,
  125, 127, 131, 135
Norway, 27, 32, 50, 70–9, 127,
  131, 158
Norwich, 102

obstacle courses, 43
officers, 8, 132–41, 146–7
Oliver, Warrant Officer Lionel, 118
Oman, 158
Oman Royal Guard, 112
Opium Wars, 8
Oslo, 76

padres, 25–6
Palace of Westminster, 152, 160
Palestine, 8, 125
pantomime, 116–20
Parachute Regiments, 82, 158
  2nd, 82
  3rd, 82
parades, 68–9
Paris, 60
Parris Island, 40, 43
Paul, St, 82
pay, 171
Pei-ho River, 62
Peking, 62, 69
Philip, Prince, 94, 177
pilots, 50–3
Pirbright, 43
Plymouth, 36, 40
Port Stanley, 16, 85, 86

Portsmouth, 128
Potential Officers Course (POC), 136
Potential Recruits Course (PRC), 32, 33–47
privatization, 37
Pyrenees, 50

Queen Elizabeth Hospital, Exeter, 118

Raiding Squadron, 3rd, 66, 68–9
Ramsgate, 103
rapid intervention force, 158
recruits, 32, 33–47, 105
refugees: Hong Kong, 61, 66
regimental music, 173
religion, 25–6
Remington M-40 rifles, 56
resignations, 32, 33, 38, 52–3, 131, 159
retirement, 149–56
rifles, 56
'Rolling Deep' exercise, 131
Romania, 158
Rome, 60
Ross, Major-General Robin J., 128–9
Royal Air Force (RAF), 50, 159
Royal Hong Kong Police, 62, 69
Royal Marine Band, 47, 68, 96–7, 101–15
Royal Marines:
    founding of, 162
    history, 161–8
    organization, 172
Royal Marines' School of Music, 98–102, 103–14, 127
Royal Military Academy, Sandhurst, 136
Royal Navy, 28, 52, 61, 64, 69, 85–7, 102–3, 134, 136, 158–9
Royal Ulster Constabulary (RUC), 19, 20, 22
Royal Yacht Britannia, 85, 109
Rules and Ordynaunces of the Warre, 94

Saillagouse, 50
St James's Park, London, 93
St Michael and All Angels, Deal, 112
Salerno, 8
Salisbury Plain, 131

Salterton, 33
samurai, 157
San Carlos Water, 82, 88, 156
Sandhurst, 40, 135, 136
Sands, Warrant Officer Tom, 56
Sarawak, 50
School of Music, Deal, 98–102, 103–14, 127
Scotland, 68
Sea King helicopters, 52, 76
Second World War, 8, 28, 82, 149–50
Sembawang, 50
Sergeants, 144–7
Shackleton, Sir Ernest, 86
Shanghai, 60
Shanghai Bank, 64
Shankill, 19
ships, 131
shooting: snipers, 54–6
Sicily, 8
Sikorsky helicopters, 88
Singapore, 50, 127, 129, 141
Sioux AH Mk1 helicopters, 50
skidoos, 76–8
Slim, Field-Marshal, 125
snipers, 54–6
snowmobiles, 76–8
Somerset, 52
Sotheby's, 150
South Armagh, 12
South Atlantic, 50, 85, 88
South China Sea, 60, 61, 62, 66, 127
South-East Asia, 60–9
Soviet Union, 7, 72–3, 125, 157, 158
Sp Company, 76
Spain, 102, 103
Sparks, Bill, 149–50
Special Air Service (SAS), 157
Special Forces Units, 150
Sri Lanka, 158
Stirling, 125
submarines, 73
Sultan, HMS, 136
survival training, 73–9
Swallow, HMS, 68
Swayne, David Brian, 155–6
Swift, HMS, 68

Tai Ping Rebellion (1850), 61
Taku Forts, 62
Tamar, HMS, 62–6

terrorism, 19–24, 101, 158
Thatcher, Margaret, 157
Third World, 158
Thompson, Brigadier, 50–2
3 Commando Brigade, 50, 72–9
Tiananmen Square, Peking, 69
Tower of London, 149
tracking, 56
Trafalgar, Battle of (1805), 102, 164
training, 156
    Arctic warfare, 72–9, 158
    musicians, 105
    new recruits, 29–47
    officers, 136–41, 146–7
    pilots, 52
    snipers, 56
    survival, 73–9
Treatise of Military Disciplin (Bland), 94
Trondheim, 50
Troop 267, 156
Troop 571, 35–6, 40, 47
Tumbledown, 85
Turflodge Estate, Belfast, 23
Turnhill Barracks, 125

Ulster, 8, 12–24, 50, 125, 127, 131, 135
Ulster Defence Regiment (UDR), 14
uniform, 35, 36, 169, 174, 175
United States of America, 125, 156, 157
United States Marine Corps (USMC), 36, 40, 43, 50, 56, 62, 72, 158–9

Vaux, Major-General Nicholas Francis, 130–1, 141
Venn Ottery, 33
Victoria Cross, 8, 164, 165, 179–82
Victoria Peak, Hong Kong, 60
Victory, HMS, 102–3
Vietnam, 61

Walker, Mel, 118
Walmer, 103
Wanchai, 60
Ward, Lieutenant Jason, 141
Warrant Officers, 144
Warsaw Pact, 73, 158
weapons, 183
Weddell Sea, 86

Wellington Barracks, 94, 96
Wellington School, 134
West Belfast, 19, 20–2
West Indies, 125, 156
Whitehall, 90–7

Whiterock, 19
Williams, Terry, 101–2
Windy Gap, 156
Wingate, Orde, 125, 157
women, 8, 27–8, 129, 159

Woods, Corporal Brent, 23–4
WRNS, 27–8, 129, 159

Yangtze River, 125
Yeovilton, 52